g photographed together for the last time as they appeared before the
d upon them. From left to right, front row: Hermann Göring (sentenced
eld Marshal Wilhelm Keitel (death): Ernst Kaltenbrunner (death): Alfred
r (death): Walther Funk (life imprisonment): and Dr Hjalmar Schacht
: (ten years imprisonment): Erich Raeder (life imprisonment): Baldur von
Franz von Papen (acquitted): Arthur Seyss-Inquart (death): Albert Speer
t): and Hans Fritzsche (acquitted).

The Nazi War Trials

The Nazi War Trials

ANDREW WALKER

POCKET ESSENTIALS

First published in 2006 by Pocket Essentials
P.O.Box 394, Harpenden, Herts, AL5 1XJ
www.pocketessentials.com

A CIP catalogue record for this book is available from the British Library.

ISBN-10: 1 903047 50 1
EAN-13: 978 1 903047 50 7

2 4 6 8 10 9 7 5 3 1

Typeset by Avocet Typeset, Chilton, Aylesbury, Bucks
Printed and bound in Great Britain by CPD Ltd, Ebbw Vale, Wales

In memory of
Betty Aileen Roberts
1916 – 2003

Acknowledgements

I am grateful for the kindness and support shown by Sarah Walsh and Nick Rennison during the writing of this book.

Contents

Introduction

One of the most extraordinary things about the Nazi War trials in Nuremberg in 1945 and 1946 was the fact that they took place at all. At the end of the most devastating war in history, victors as well as vanquished were exhausted. Much of Europe was in ruins. Germany itself was a virtual waste-land and many of its people were close to starvation. In this context, the fact that a tribunal was convened and that, over a period of more than a year, those leading Nazis who had survived and been captured were tried for war crimes and crimes against humanity is astonishing enough. Yet, the trials themselves were unprecedented. Never before had nations in victory attempted to hold the leaders of the defeated nation to legal account. The challenges faced by those who established the tribunal were enormous. The international law under which the men were tried was debatable. The argument that the trial was vengeance masquerading as jus-tice was one that was heard from its beginning. To prove, as Rebecca West wrote, that 'victors can so rise above the ordi-nary limitations of human nature as to be able to try fairly the foes they vanquished, by submitting themselves to the restraints of law' would be no easy task.

From the very beginning the Nuremberg Trial was about much more than the individual fates of the men who stood trial. It became the focus of desires for a post-war settlement in Europe that would ensure lasting peace and that would exorcise the horrors of the previous six years. It embodied hopes that solutions could be found to problems of international conflict which had plagued the continent for centuries. Again in the words of Rebecca West, it could 'warn all future war-mongers that law can at last pursue them into peace and thus give humanity a new defence against them'. In this sense, the Nazi War Trials can be seen as one of the most significant events of the twentieth century.

This book is primarily an attempt to provide a clear and accurate précis of what happened at Nuremberg between 20 November 1945, when the trial began, and 16 October 1946, when sentence was carried out on those men convicted by the tribunal. It identifies each of the defendants, summarises the charges against each of them and gives a brief account of the prosecution and defence speeches, the judgement, the sentencing and the carrying out of the sentences. It also looks at the cases the Allies made against various key organisations within the Nazi state. To set the trials in context, the book examines the debate amongst the Allies before the war ended about what form judgement on the Nazis would take and looks briefly at events after they were concluded. At a time when the war crimes court in The Hague still pursues men involved in the Balkans War and when the trial of Saddam Hussein in Iraq is underway, the Nuremberg Trial has a renewed relevance and this book endeavours to show why.

Preliminaries

'The wrongs which we seek to condemn and punish have been so calculated, so malignant, and so devastating, that civilization cannot tolerate their being ignored, because it cannot survive their being repeated. That four great nations, flushed with victory and stung with injury stay the hand of vengeance and voluntarily submit their captive enemies to the judgment of the law is one of the most significant tributes that Power has ever paid to Reason.'

Robert H Jackson, Opening Address for the United States, November 21st 1945

Background to the Trial

As the Allies began their advance upon Germany on two fronts in 1944, the fate of the top ranking Nazi leaders was being hotly debated. The one abiding aim for all parties was to avoid the travesty of justice that had followed Germany's surrender in 1918. Then the German government had been charged with the prosecution of those men accused of war crimes. After the punitive Treaty of Versailles, the will to pander to the demands of the Allies was clearly lacking, and the Kaiser was able to live out his days in peaceable exile in the Netherlands. Other cases were pursued with no more vigour: out of the 45 cases set for trial, only 12 came to court, and from them only six men were convicted.

In 1944 then, the Allies had a precedent to avoid, but little more of substance. As early as October 1941 Churchill and Roosevelt had declared that the punishment of crimes committed by the Nazis was a major goal of the war. In 1943 three German officers were found guilty by the Soviets and shot. After D-Day, American and British troops were increasingly likely to apprehend such people and a unified protocol was urgently required. By Churchill's own account, the issue had been encapsulated in a bizarre exchange between the three leaders at Teheran in 1943. Stalin stated his opinion that justice would be served by the execution of 50,000 Nazis. Churchill remonstrated that he would sooner be taken out into the garden himself and shot than countenance such an idea. Roosevelt, mediating between his two fellow leaders, came up with the somewhat ghoulish compromise that 49,000 should suffice. Churchill stormed out of the room, only to return when Stalin assured him that the remark was made in jest. Thus Churchill painted a scene of the British sense of justice outraged by Soviet barbarity, with only the pragmatism of the Americans to unite them.

Yet the reality was not quite so convenient. It was Churchill who was set on the idea of summary justice, fearing that a long drawn out trial would provide an unwelcome opportunity for the Nazi leadership to garner sympathy. In notes made by the deputy cabinet secretary (made public only in 2006), it's clear Churchill proposed execution for Hitler, 'Instrument – electric chair, for gangsters, no doubt available on lease-lend'. He also proposed that a list of 'grand criminals' be drawn up, and these men 'be shot as soon as they were caught and their identity established'. A surprising stickler for propriety was Stalin, who, not known to be troubled by the concept of a trial taking any longer than he wished, counselled against the absence of a court hearing and warned that this would leave the Allies open to accusations of vindictiveness. The British Ambassador in Moscow caught the Soviet attitude perfectly when he demurred to Stalin, 'I am sure that the political decision that Mr Churchill has in mind will be accompanied by all the necessary formalities'.

The Americans too had their disagreements. For a large part of the war, their country was far removed from the direct horror of Nazi aggression on mainland Europe and there was little public outrage until the massacre of seventy American prisoners-of-war by SS troops at Malmédy in December 1944. The subsequent clamour for vengeance strengthened the hand of Henry Morgenthau, the Secretary of the Treasury. His extreme plan for post-war Germany called for the country to be permanently stripped of its means to wage war by reducing it to the level of an agricultural society. In his view, the leading Nazis were clearly guilty of murder and should be summarily executed. Opposed to these draconian measures was the Secretary of War, Henry Stimson, who believed that the wealth and stability of Germany were vital to the success of post-war Europe. For him, establishing the guilt of the Nazi leadership before an international court would be an essential part of the process of rehabilitating the German people. Such a trial would also serve the unashamedly idealistic aim of establishing a legal precedent to deter men from waging war in the future.

Both men vied for the ear of the dying President. Roosevelt, although characteristically disposed to deferring the decision for as long as possible, was personally inclined to favour the severe measures recommended by Morgenthau. Until Roosevelt's death in April 1945, Stimson appeared to be losing the battle. Roosevelt's successor, Harry Truman, however, enthusiastically backed Stimson's proposal, and its sudden elevation to policy led to the acceptance of the principle of a trial by the Allied powers at the founding conference of the United Nations in May of that year.

Yet much remained to be decided. Truman appointed Supreme Court Justice Robert H Jackson 'chief of counsel for the prosecution of Axis criminality'. Jackson was a brilliant and passionate lawyer, whose distinguished career was unusual in that his admission to the bar was obtained by serving an apprenticeship rather than by obtaining a law school degree. Jackson inherited the concept of the trial proposed by Lieutenant Colonel Murray Bernays, an attorney in the War Department. Bernays had suggested invoking the law of conspiracy to try the career of the Third Reich as one vast pre-meditated criminal enterprise. Not only would this enable a single trial to address the vast number of individual outrages, but it would also hold accountable the Nazi leaders, who might otherwise claim that they had not personally executed civilians or burnt down villages. A similar catch-all proposal in Bernays' plan was to charge organisations with crimes. Thus, finding the SS as a whole guilty of criminal activity, for example, would mean that trials against individuals could proceed easily on the basis of their membership of it.

Jurists from the four major Allied powers met in London in July to establish the legal mechanisms for such a trial. It is worth stressing the point that all this had to be done from scratch, as there were simply no precedents in international law for the trial of war criminals. Jackson and the American team had provided the basic concept of the trial, but national differences were not easily overcome. The law of conspiracy had been used with great success against organised crime and fraudulent businesses in America, but had no basis in Continental or Soviet law. Even the adversarial nature of the Anglo-Saxon system was alien to the French representatives. The eventual structure of the court was therefore a necessary hybrid. Opposing lawyers would present cases for the prosecution and the defence, as in the Anglo-Saxon model, but a panel of four judges would pass judgement, with four alternates sitting in reserve. Even the decision that a conviction would require a vote of at least three to one was reached in the face of appalled protests from the Soviet delegation.

Less easily overcome were grave objections to the legality of the trial itself. By defining the crimes after the event, the Allies risked creating 'ex post facto' law. The Nazis may well have conspired to wage aggressive war, but when they had done so, however immoral it was, it was not illegal. Jackson's argument was pragmatic, if not entirely persuasive. 'Let's not be derailed by legal hair-splitters', he intoned, 'Aren't murder, torture, and enslavement crimes recognized by all civilized people?' This justification indirectly raised the other uncomfortable point that the defence lawyers might make. Just as the Axis forces had committed atrocities, so had the Allies. The Soviets, who would be sitting in judgement on the Nazi leadership, had themselves invaded Poland in 1939, shortly after the Germans. The representatives at the conference were at pains to avoid the trial appearing simply as victor's justice, but it was an undeniable fact that the Nazis were on trial because they were on the losing side. This argument of 'tu quoque' ('you also') could not be allowed to jeopardise the trial, and the way around it was uncompromising: the court would render any line of defence based on this argument inadmissible.

After six weeks of often exasperating legal wrangling, the Charter of the International Military Tribunal was signed. Article 6 set out the Tribunal's power to try those charged with committing any of four crimes: Crimes against Peace, War Crimes, Crimes against Humanity and Engaging in a Common Plan or Conspiracy for the accomplishment of any of these.

The Defendants

The question of who was to stand trial caused as much debate and deal-making among the Allied powers as any of the previous issues. Again the Americans were to the fore, not least because the majority of the candidates for trial had been astute enough to fall into their hands rather than those of the Russians. The most prominent Nazi still alive was the flamboyant Reichsmarschall, Herman Göring. Despite having been stripped of office in Hitler's last act before his suicide, Göring went into captivity with typically arrogant bravado. When he arrived at the detention centre in the resort hotel of Bad Mondorf, he had with him his valet and a sixteen-piece set of matching luggage. Contained in the luggage were over 20,000 paracodeine tablets, to which he was addicted. Second only to Göring in prominence was Rudolf Hess, the deputy leader of the Nazi party, who had flown to Scotland in 1941 in a bizarre attempt to broker peace between Britain and Germany. Having been in Allied captivity since then, his inclusion for trial was a clear signal by the Allies that the entire career of the Third Reich was within the remit of the Tribunal's charter.

Hitler's successor as Führer, Grand Admiral Karl Dönitz, had set up a short-lived government in Flensburg, from where he had sent the chief of Wehrmacht operations, Colonel General Alfred Jodl, to negotiate surrender to the Americans. Both men were taken into custody at Flensburg after the surrender, together with the Chief of Staff of the armed forces, Field Marshal Wilhelm Keitel, Hitler's former Armaments Minister Albert Speer, and the foremost philosopher of Nazism, Alfred Rosenberg.

The Allies were clearly motivated in their choice of defendants by a desire to represent the full compass of Nazi rule and to give the widest possible range of injured parties the sense that justice would be done. Defendants with geographical responsibilities included Hans Frank, Governor-General of occupied Poland, Arthur Seyss-Inquart, Reich commissioner for the Netherlands, and Minister of the Interior, Wilhelm Frick. The role that management of the economy played in Hitler's rise to power was indicated by the inclusion on the indictment of Hjalmar Schacht, former head of the Reichsbank, and Walther Funk, Reich Minister of Economics. With an eye to the charge of conspiracy, three diplomats were also indicted: Joachim von Ribbentrop, Hitler's Foreign Minister, his predecessor Constantin von

Neurath, and the former Reich chancellor, Franz von Papen. Less grand functionaries were Fritz Sauckel, Reich Director of Labour, and Ernst Kaltenbrunner, the fearsome chief of the Reich Central Security Office.

Deprived of the chance to indict Hitler's Propaganda Minister, Joseph Goebbels, by his suicide, the Allies called other men to account for the dissemination of Nazi culture. Baldur von Schirach had been Head of Hitler Youth from 1933 to 1940; Julius Streicher had been editor of the anti-semitic paper 'Der Stürmer'. Both were named on the indictment. Largely because he was one of only two likely candidates held by the Soviets, the propagandist and broad-caster Hans Fritzsche was also included. The other Soviet contribution to the list was Erich Raeder, head of the navy until 1943.

In addition to these twenty-one, three men were named on the indictment but did not appear before the International Military Tribunal at Nuremberg. Hitler's Private Secretary Martin Bormann was tried 'in absentia', although there were several reports that he had died trying to escape from Hitler's bunker in Berlin. The industrialist Gustav Krupp von Bohlen und Halbach was pronounced too senile to stand trial. Anxious to represent German industry on the indictment, Jackson tried to have him replaced at the trial by his son Alfred who had been in charge of Krupps' weapons production during the war. Much to Jackson's cha-grin the motion was thrown out of court. The third missing man was Robert Ley, the alcoholic leader of the Labour Front, who committed suicide in his cell before the trial started.

Preparations for the Trial

Before the trial could commence, there were certain practicalities which had to be settled. Where were the proceedings to take place? How, and where, were the prisoners to be held in custody? How were they to be defended? How was the courtroom to be laid out? How was it to be reported and recorded? In this trial, the most basic of questions – which would simply not arise in ordinary proceedings, governed by precedent and the custom of centuries – had to be answered.

That the trial had to take place in Germany was not in doubt. Justice had to be seen to be done in the country in whose name the defendants had held power, not in the capital of one of the victorious nations. Berlin was the obvious choice for a venue, and indeed the Russians (unsurprisingly) argued vociferously that it should take place there, but the city was in rubble, it was overcrowded and its limited resources were already stretched to the limits. An American general suggested Nuremberg. The city, with its huge rallies, had had a central role in Nazi propaganda and, by chance, some of its major buildings, despite the enormous damage inflicted by Allied bombing, were still intact. The Palace of Justice was still standing and so too was the jail which was linked directly to the court. Most importantly for the Americans, it was in a part of Germany they controlled. Eventually, the Russians conceded and, although Berlin was named formally as the 'permanent seat of the Tribunal', Nuremberg was to be the site of the trial.

The first formal session of the Tribunal took place (in Berlin) on 18 October 1945. The indictments of those who would face the court were presented and a date set for the trial to begin – 20 November. The defendants, by now ensconced in Nuremberg jail under the guardianship of an American colonel named Burton C. Andrus, were served with the indictment on 19 October. The time had come for them to choose lawyers to present their defence cases in the forthcoming trial. Only Dönitz, who had heard of a naval officer and lawyer called Otto Kranzbuehler, was prepared and, more than a week later, half of the defendants were still without counsel. The process of ensuring that all the prisoners had legal representation proved a slow one but, despite the concerns of both prosecution and defendants, it eventually reached a satisfactory conclusion. Göring, originally scornful of the very idea that German lawyers could be persuaded to take part in the proceedings, was pleased with his own choice of a judge from Kiel called Stahmer. Since Stahmer was quoted as saying that he was 'not finding it difficult to persuade himself of Göring's innocence' (a task very nearly everybody else in Germany would have found exceedingly difficult), the Reichsmarschall's pleasure is understandable. Some of the defence lawyers were later to prove major irritations to the court. Of von Papen's counsel, Kuboschok, the judge Norman Birkett wrote that, 'he is not exactly to be described as a windbag, because that implies some powers of rhetoric and possible eloquence. Of these qualities this man is strikingly bereft.' However, despite the knowledge that some of the defence lawyers were undoubtedly former Nazis, the Tribunal only stepped in to veto one defendant's choice of counsel. Rosenberg requested that he should be defended by his fellow prisoner Hans Frank, but the prospect of Frank zig-zagging between the dock and the lawyers' lectern throughout the trial was not one the Tribunal was prepared to contemplate. Rosenberg was obliged to look elsewhere.

As the task of finding defence lawyers for them went ahead, the prisoners settled into the routine which Andrus had devised for them. Much of their time was spent alone. Just about the only opportunity to chat to one another came in the daily half-hour of exercise in the prison yard. For the rest of the day, the men were confined to their cells with little to do but read and write letters. Andrus was not unaware of the dangers of keeping his prisoners largely unoccupied – 'a guy could go nuts,' he wrote, 'sitting in a little cell with what some of these boys have got on their minds' – but he needed to keep them under almost permanent surveillance. After Ley's suicide on 25 October, restrictions on the men only became more severe. Andrus was, at heart, a decent and humane man but he was determined that he should lose noone else under his care and the surveillance was stepped up several degrees. Just about the only relief from the deadening routine was provided by visits from doctors and psychiatrists. Gustav Gilbert, the prison psychologist, asked the men to take a series of intelligence tests and many enjoyed doing them. Göring, in particular, behaved 'like a bright, egotistical schoolboy, anxious to show off before the teacher' and his good humour was only spoiled when he was told that he had come third in the IQ ratings behind Schacht and Seyss-Inquart. All the prisoners tested higher than average. Sauckel, Kaltenbrunner and Streicher scored lowest.

The men were also able to record their responses to the indictment. Reactions varied wildly. Streicher, still caught in the web of his own fantasies about global conspiracy, noted that, 'This trial is a triumph of World Jewry'. Göring, convinced that the result of the trial was a foregone conclusion, commented that 'the victor will always be the judge and the vanquished the accused'. Hess claimed he could remember little, if anything, of the past. The soldiers among the defendants fell back on the arguments that they had obeyed orders, that to do so was a soldier's duty and that they had known nothing of the terrible crimes committed by the regime they served. Only a small number of the men seemed willing to acknowledge any justice in the trial. Von Schirach was prepared to admit that, 'the whole misfortune comes from racial politics.' Speer went even further, writing that, 'The trial is necessary. There is a common responsibility for such horrible crimes even in an authoritarian system.'

As the defendants faced up to the indictment, the apparatus for judging their 'common responsibility' for the crimes was being established. Throughout November, the judges and prosecuting counsel began to arrive in Nuremberg. The task of finding billets for them and for the support staff, hundreds strong, which they brought with them was undertaken. Documents that would be put before the court were gathered, analysed and translated. Last-minute legal problems were addressed. Were Hess and Streicher, for instance, sane enough to be tried? Finally, and despite late requests from the French and the Russians that proceedings should be delayed, the trial that was to judge not only individual defendants but the crimes of an entire regime was ready to begin.

The Trial: Prosecution Case

The Trial Begins

The opening of the trial on 20 November 1945 was preceded by frantic last-minute manoeuvres. The French and Soviet delegations both wanted the trial delayed. The Soviets claimed that Rudenko, the head of their prosecution team, had been struck down with malaria. According to the British Foreign Office this was malaria 'of the diplomatic variety'. The defence lawyers then jointly filed a motion challenging the validity of the Tribunal, contesting that war had not been outlawed by any recognised international law. The American and British camps were determined that the trial start on time. The defence motion was rejected by invoking Article Three of the Charter, which ruled out any challenges to its authority. The French and Soviets backed down after threats to publicise their delaying tactics and Rudenko enjoyed a startling and welcome recovery from his malaria.

The trial started amid intense security. Rumours of an attempt to free the defendants by a group of Bavarian Nazis had been passed to the Allies by a young woman working in the court library, who happened to be the niece of the late Field Marshal Erwin Rommel. Those filing into the courtroom on that bright Tuesday morning had to pass numerous

gun emplacements and check points. The extraordinary significance of the trial drew the cream of the world's press
from 23 countries. CBS had sent Howard Smith and William
Shirer, the novelist John Dos Passos was there, reporting for
Life magazine, and the *New Yorker* magazine was represented
by Janet Flanner and Rebecca West.

The sight that greeted these journalists was one of calculated solemnity. The walls of the courtroom were panelled
in dark oak, and dark green curtains were hung over the
windows. The dock consisted of two wooden benches
behind a low partition and was situated directly opposite the
dais on which the judges would sit. The commandant of the
prison, Burton Andrus, had filled the courtroom with his
most impressive guards, their uniforms bearing the coat of
arms designed by himself. They wore gleaming white hel-
mets and webbing and were all armed with white truncheons (only the most observant spectator would spot that
these were actually sawn-off mop handles). The whole scene
was lit by garish fluorescent lighting, bright enough to
accommodate the film cameras that were present behind a
sound-proof screen.

The trial began at 10 o'clock in the morning with the
statement by the President, Sir Geoffrey Lawrence, calling
on all participants in the trial, 'to discharge their duties
without fear or favour, in accordance with the sacred princi-
ples of law and justice.' The reading of the indictment followed. This was very much a formality since the defendants
had received copies of the indictment over a month previously. The reading lasted nearly a day and a half and, if nothing else, provided those present with a good chance to
analyse the men in the dock. Göring, Keitel and Jodl wore

their uniforms, which were much less impressive than they might have been because they had been stripped of all insignia. The rest of the defendants all wore dark suits, with the exception of Frick, who sported an outlandish check jacket. Göring sat through the reading with an expression of studied boredom, Ribbentrop was seen to be sweating profusely and Walther Funk sobbed intermittently. Those expecting to see the supermen who had engineered the rise of the Thousand Year Reich felt severe disappointment. As William Shirer noted in his diary, 'Shorn of the power and the glory and the glittering trappings of Nazidom, how little and mean and mediocre they look'.

The following day the defendants were required to enter their pleas in response to the indictment. Göring attempted to make a statement but was cut short by Lawrence who insisted on a simple plea of 'guilty' or 'not guilty'. This seemed to provide swift reassurance to those critics of the trial who had feared that it would provide too easy a platform for Nazi propaganda but, in truth, it merely highlighted Justice Lawrence's strict legal rectitude. Later, he would freely allow the defendants their say. Göring's statement was issued to the press, however, and prefigures the aggressive line of defence he was to pursue later in the trial: 'I must... most strongly reject the accusation that my acts, for which I accept full responsibility, should be described as criminal. I must also reject the acceptance by me of responsibility for the acts of other persons which were not known to me'. All defendants denied that they were guilty as charged, and Hess's curt 'Nein' was dryly interpreted by Lawrence as a plea of 'not guilty', which led to a rare outburst of laughter in the courtroom.

The American and British Cases

An air of anticipation was felt as Robert Jackson stepped up to open the prosecution case for the United States. Jackson was to have his critics as a cross-examiner and man-manager but there was no doubt that here he was in his element. His opening address reached oratorical heights few present had heard before in a court of law. In acknowledging immediately that the Tribunal itself was 'novel and experimental', Jackson was able to emphasise what an achievement it was that it existed at all.

'Yet less than eight months ago today the courtroom in which you sit was an enemy fortress in the hands of SS troops. Less than eight months ago nearly all our witness and documents were in enemy hands. The law had not been codified, no procedures had been established, no tribunal was in existence, no usable courthouse stood here, none of the hundreds of tons of official German documents had been examined, no prosecuting staff had been assembled, nearly all of the present defendants were at large, and the four prosecuting powers had not yet joined in common cause to try them.'

He was equally candid in tackling the criticism that the trial would be no more than a case of victors' justice and, in doing so, touched upon the idealism that underpinned so much thinking in the immediate aftermath of the war.

'The former high station of these defendants, the notoriety of their acts, and the adaptability of their conduct to provoke retaliation make it hard to distinguish between a just and measured retribution and the unthinking cry for vengeance which arises from the anguish of war... We must summon such detachment and intellectual integrity to our task that this Trial will commend itself to posterity as fulfilling Humanity's aspirations to do justice.'

The core of Jackson's speech set out the United States's case that a conspiratorial plan underlay every aspect of Nazi criminality. An outline of the history of the Nazi party demonstrated that the tools of repression were honed against their political opponents within Germany. Communists, trade unionists, figureheads in the Church and the German Jews were the first victims of Nazi concentration camps. For Jackson, this was the necessary prelude to the aggression aimed at the rest of Europe. Hitler's own words, minuted by Friedrich Hossbach at a conference in 1937 attended by four of the defendants, set out the need for *lebensraum* or 'living space' to be acquired for the German people. 'The German problem can be solved only by way of force', quoted Jackson. Nor was this view restricted to the Führer. Jackson also quoted a naval memorandum of 1939: 'If decisive successes are to be expected from any measure considered as a war necessity, it must be carried through even if it is not in agreement with international law'.

By quoting from captured documents, Jackson gave the first indications of what was to be his aim throughout the trial – to damn the Nazis with their own words. This tactic proved chilling when Jackson moved to the subject of war crimes. He read from the report of SS General Jürgen Stroop on the destruction of the Warsaw ghetto.

'Jews... frequently remained in the burning buildings and jumped out of the windows only when the heat became unbearable. They then tried to crawl with broken bones across the street.'

In Russia the Einsatzgruppen, or SS special action groups, had followed the advancing army, murdering political commissars and Jewish civilians without compunction. Jackson revealed that the preferred technique was to load victims into gas vans, which were then driven to secluded sites. A concern of an SS officer was that this required dry conditions, 'since those to be executed become frantic ... such vans become immobilised in wet weather'.

The triumph of Jackson's speech was to make palpable the crimes for which the twenty-one rather shabby defendants were on trial. He received immediate praise in the press and from his colleagues. Forty-eight years later a leading member of the American prosecution team reflected that, 'Jackson had started this great trial at a level of force, feeling, and dignity which, I believe, no other man could have attained.'

It was inevitable that, after such a grandiloquent opening, the ensuing presentation of the American case would seem something of an anti-climax. Sessions on the evidentiary background of the case and the early stages of Nazi conspiracy were worthy rather than spectacular. Moreover, an enormous drawback of the documentary approach came to light when Major Frank Wallis was presenting evidence on 'the aims of the Nazi party and their doctrinal techniques'. The American team had prepared briefs which summarised the mass of documentary evidence, and these were handed over to the Tribunal clerk. Lawrence interrupted proceedings to ask whether there were copies for the Defense Counsel. Wallis replied that, according to agreed procedure, six copies had been placed in the Defendant's Document Room. Lawrence stated the Tribunal's opinion that this was insufficient and that the Defense Counsel should each be given a copy. Such a view was hardly unreasonable given that all the defendants (including the five organisations) had been indicted on the count of conspiracy. Claims by the chief of documents Storey that the logistical problems of wider access to the documents were insurmountable had some validity, and his staff had indeed been working under tremendous strain. His credibility was strained, however, when it was revealed that, in one instance, the Defense had received five copies of a document and 250 copies had gone to the press.

This method of presenting evidence presented further problems to the trial. The American prosecutors would effectively substantiate their claims about Nazi conspiratorial aims by quoting the reference number to a mass of papers and then passing them over. Not only did this make for dull courtroom drama, it also meant that the sequence of events outlined by the Prosecution was almost impossible for most people in the court to follow. On 26 November, less than a week into the trial, the Tribunal had no choice but to introduce new rules regarding the presentation of documentary evidence. Henceforth, and until translation and copying facilities were improved, all evidence had to be read aloud and thus pass into the record by means of the simultaneous translation system. Whilst this measure undoubtedly made the proceedings fairer and clearer to follow, it slowed the progress of the Prosecution case to a crawl. Jackson was left in no doubt by the press coverage that his cherished trial was getting bogged down.

In the afternoon session on Thursday 29 November, all this was to change. James Donovan offered into evidence document number 2430 PS, a motion picture called 'Nazi Concentration Camps'. The noted Hollywood director George Stevens had produced the film, for the most part a compilation of footage taken by military photographers as the Allied armies liberated the camps in their advance across Europe. In the courtroom the curtains were drawn and the lights lowered, with the exception of a single spotlight picking out the defendants.

Today, it has to be recognised that the stark horror of such black-and-white images has been blunted by both the familiarity and the distance afforded by the passage of nearly fifty years. This was not the case in November 1945. In the words of the historian Robert E. Conot, 'the screen filled with images of skeletal men and women, crematoria and gas chambers, the scarred and disfigured bodies of women who had survived medical experiments, mound upon mound of cadavers whose sticklike arms and legs gave the appearance of jumbled piles of driftwood... and tractors pushing the dead into mass graves like contaminated jetsam'. Few in the courtroom had ever had cause even to imagine such atrocities. Jackson himself had not been alone, amongst Americans in particular, in regarding the gruesome rumours emanating from mainland Europe during the war with scepticism. Now, over the whir of the projector, came sobs of revulsion as many of the onlookers realised that the worst they had feared was the least that had happened. As soon as the film had ended, Justice Lawrence hurriedly left the courtroom without adjourning the session.

Understandably, many present during the film preferred to watch the faces of the defendants rather than look at the film. The prison psychiatrists, Major Kelley and Lieutenant

Gilbert, noted the reactions of the men in the dock. Ribbentrop, Schacht, and von Papen turned their backs on the screen. Of the military men, Keitel mopped his face continually and Dönitz covered his eyes. Hess was seen to be staring intently at the images, whilst Streicher, the most virulently anti-semitic of the defendants, leant forward, nodding his head. Later that day, the defendants were visited in their cells to elicit further responses. Keitel blamed 'those dirty SS swine'. Jodl, Dönitz, Sauckel, and Neurath all denied knowing that such things had happened, but a distraught Hans Frank, 'Butcher of Poland', would have none of it. 'Don't let anyone tell you they had no idea! Everybody sensed that there was something horribly wrong with this system, even if we didn't know all the details. They didn't want to know! It was too comfortable to live on the system, to support our families in royal style, and to believe that it was all right.' Göring, too, was able to place the contents of the film in perspective. Having been the star of the morning session as the trial covered the invasion of Austria, he concluded irritably, 'And then they showed that awful film, and it just spoiled everything'.

Jackson then capitalised on the dramatic impact of the film by calling the first witness for the prosecution. To the witness stand came the tall, cadaverous figure of Major General Erwin Lahousen. Lahousen had been an Intelligence Officer in the Austrian army. After the peaceful reoccupation of Austria, he was transferred to the Abwehr, the intelligence arm of the German army. As Executive Officer to the Abwehr chief, Admiral Wilhelm Canaris, Lahousen had been at the very centre of affairs. He had witnessed the decision-making process very often and was thus able to reveal the extent of knowledge and responsibility amongst the defendants.

All the accused were horrified by the appearance of a serving officer as a witness for the prosecution, not least because, unlike many of the witnesses to follow, Lahousen had no case to answer himself. His appearance could not be attributed to self-interest. His main motive appeared to be retribution for the execution of Canaris after the unsuccessful attempt on Hitler's life in 1944. Göring certainly saw it that way, referring contemptuously to Lahousen as, 'that traitor: that's one we forgot on 20 July'.

Keitel had good reason to be anxious, as Lahousen recounted an attack on the radio station at Gleiwitz in 1939. In a plot hatched by the SS, German troops faked an attack on their own station, leaving behind dead concentration camp internees dressed in Polish army uniforms. Hitler then used the apparent assault as a pretext for launching the invasion of Poland. Lahousen had been given the task by Canaris of obtaining the Polish uniforms for the deception, and he could prove that Canaris in turn had received his orders from Keitel.

Just as discomfiting was the evidence that, during the invasion of France, Keitel had issued an order for the capture and assassination of two fugitive French generals. Issuing orders that led to unspeakable brutality and suffering were interpreted by the defendants as following one's duty. An attack on the person of a general, even an enemy one, was seen as a grave transgression of the code of the Prussian officer corps. During the lunchtime recess that day, Keitel duly received the cold shoulder from Dönitz, Raeder and Jodl.

Cross-examination of Lahousen by the counsel for the defence showed how totally unfamiliar the German lawyers were with this particular legal technique. The long, circuitous questions gave Lahousen ample opportunity to prepare his replies and, in one astonishing instance, even Göring was visibly exasperated. If Lahousen had believed Keitel's orders to be 'murderous', and therefore criminal, asked Dr von der Lippe, why had he not reported them to the police? The line of argument adopted was indicative of the overall defence strategy throughout the trial. The facts presented during the prosecution case could rarely be challenged or repudiated, because one of the strengths of the documentary approach was that most of the evidence came from the written reports of the Nazis themselves. The preferred tack was to argue that it was not a particular defendant, but rather Hitler or some other official, who was responsible for the matter in question and that the defendant had either no hand in it or had made an effort to ameliorate its consequences.

After Lahousen had left the stand on 30 November, Justice Lawrence announced that the court would meet in private session to discuss a pressing legal matter. The bizarre behaviour of Rudolf Hess – his constant goose-stepping in the exercise yard and his apparent inability to recognise even as old a comrade as Göring – had been causing the judges concern. In the courtroom, it seemed to Rebecca West that, 'he looked as if his mind had no surface, as if every part of it had been blasted away except the depth where the nightmares live'. A medical panel had, upon investigation, concluded that Hess was legally sane but suffered from hysterical amnesia.

Jackson was of the view that Hess was, 'in the volunteer class with his amnesia'. The British prosecutor David Maxwell-Fyfe put forward a convoluted argument on the legal distinction between insanity and amnesia, a performance the American judge, Francis Biddle, noted as, 'damned lawyer's bull at first blush'. Hess's counsel, Gunter von Rohrscheidt, rose and began to explain his belief that his client was not fit to stand trial. His amnesia, the argument went, meant that he could not adequately follow the proceedings in court, and was unable to draw on his own recollections to challenge the prosecution case. As Rohrscheidt spoke, Hess grew increasingly agitated. He passed a scribbled note, which Rohrscheidt read but appeared to ignore. Hess then tried to draw the attention of the judges by waving wildly. Justice Lawrence eventually asked that Hess be allowed to speak. Eerily calm and composed, the defendant rose to address the court.

'Henceforth my memory will again respond to the outside world. The reasons for simulating loss of memory were of a tactical nature. Only my ability to concentrate is, in fact, somewhat reduced. But my capacity to follow the trial, to defend myself, to put questions to witnesses, or to answer questions myself is not affected thereby... I also simulated loss of memory in consultations with my officially appointed defense counsel. He has, therefore, represented me in good faith.'

There followed a moment of astonished silence, broken by a wave of unbridled laughter. Lawrence adjourned the court in uproar and the assembled journalists scrambled to report the extraordinary story. In the frenzy of speculation that followed, Captain Gilbert provided the most telling insight. He had approached Hess during a recess and warned him that, if he were found unfit to stand trial, he would be removed from the prison and the company of his co-defendants. Hess had looked troubled. He had spent almost the entire war in a British prison and the trial at Nuremberg had put him back with old comrades, talking in his native language. Gilbert claimed that the realisation that he might lose this privilege made Hess snap out of one form of hysterical amnesia. However, the assertion that he had simulated loss of memory was itself another manifestation of his illness. In the words of a forthright headline of the day, 'Hess Nuts. Fake Story Fake, says Nuremberg Psychologist'.

The prosecution case continued with the portion of the conspiracy charge dealing with crimes against humanity. A former member of the FBI, Thomas Dodd, made a two-day presentation on the Nazi forced labour programme. Throughout the war, 4.75 million foreign workers were forced to work in support of the German economy. The methods were brutal but caused few qualms. Hans Frank had noted in his diary that he had, 'no objections at all to the rubbish, capable of work yet often loitering about, being snatched from the streets'. Dodd revealed that the daily rations in a typical arms factory comprised a cup of tea at 4 o'clock in the morning, followed by a bowl of soup and two slices of bread when the shift ended 14 hours later.

Although Dodd quoted Frank, Keitel, Rosenberg and Seyss-Inquart during this presentation, the defendants with the most to lose were Albert Speer and Fritz Sauckel. Albert Speer had been appointed Reich Minister for Arms and Production in 1942. Frustrated by the geographical and hierarchical rivalries between Nazi officials, Speer had suggested that someone should be put in overall charge of supplying the manpower needs of the German economy. Sauckel was duly appointed Plenipotentiary-General for Labour Mobilization. Speer would determine how many workers were needed in the different areas of production and Sauckel would be responsible for rounding up the workforce. It was not a happy relationship, with Speer showing thinly disguised contempt for Sauckel's inefficiency. Sauckel was sufficiently tormented by his job to stow away in a U-Boat, pleading with its captain to employ him in any role rather than return him to land. Which of the two men shouldered the most responsibility – Speer the slave driver or Sauckel the slave trader – was a moot point. Airey Neave, the officer who had served both men their indictments, feared that the issue might come down to class. Would the judges show instinctive preference for the urbane and clubbable Speer rather than the 'unattractive and plebeian' Sauckel?

The defendants had an unexpected respite from their troubles on 11 December, when a second film was offered into evidence. Entitled 'The Nazi Plan', it was a compilation of German footage illustrating the rise to power of the Nazi party and its rule up until 1944. It was an opportunity for the defendants to remember what, for them, were happier times. Hess was pictured in the full flight of a speech, screaming, 'The Party is the Führer and the Führer is Germany'. Speer warmed to the sight of the Nuremberg Rally of 1934, his masterpiece of mass theatre filmed by Leni Riefenstahl. Schacht beamed proudly as the documentary set out the dramatic economic recovery which had powered the Nazi preparations for war. Schirach was in raptures at the sight of marching ranks of Hitler Youth.

THE TRIAL: PROSECUTION CASE

Overjoyed at the sight of Hitler on the screen, raising himself to the heights of oratorical frenzy, Göring exclaimed to Hess, his neighbour in the dock, 'Justice Jackson will want to join the Party now!'

For many in the courtroom, it was a scene from another film shown that day that had the deepest impact. It showed the trial of suspects following the unsuccessful attempt on Hitler's life in July 1944. Physically dragged before the judge, suspects stood helplessly, clutching at their beltless trousers. 'Are you collapsing under the stress of your own vulgarity, you filthy rogue?' screamed Judge Roland Freisler at an army officer who had faltered whilst attempting to describe murders he had witnessed in Poland. Nearly 200 Germans were tried before Peoples' Courts, some in the very same room in which the present trial was taking place. They met their various deaths by firing squad, axe and slow strangulation with piano wire. Few in the court failed to make the obvious comparison with the treatment accorded the current defendants.

If the film had not already dampened spirits in the dock, Dodd had prepared a further, chilling blow. On 13 December, a table was laid out in the courtroom on which several items were covered by a white sheet. Entering into the evidence USA exhibit 253, Dodd unveiled a collection of pale, leathery objects. The more sharp-eyed in the room spotted that all the objects featured darker patterns which, Dodd explained, were tattoos. Karl Koch, the commandant of Buchenwald concentration camp, had selected prisoners with interesting tattoos to be murdered. The tattoos were then removed from the victims and the resulting pieces of skin were handed over to Koch's wife, 'who had them fashioned into lampshades and other ornamental household articles'. Exhibit 254 was a shrivelled nut-like object, the size of an orange. This, Dodd revealed, was the head of a Polish officer who had been hanged for having a sexual encounter with a German woman. Having dried and shrunken it to its present size, Koch had used it as a paperweight.

The defense counsel for Ernst Kaltenbrunner attempted to challenge the evidence by pointing out the prosecution's omission of the fact that an SS court had sentenced Karl Koch to death in 1944. The prosecution were temporarily wrong-footed by this news, but the truth eventually came to light. The crimes for which Koch's peers felt he must pay with his life were the embezzlement of SS funds and the killing of a member of the Nazi party.

Unwittingly, the SS were to provide another hammer blow to the defendants' hopes. A film that had been shot by an amateur SS photographer was shown to the court. Damaged by fire, and lasting only ninety seconds, the footage was shown in slow motion. Sitting in the public gallery, the journalist Janet Flanner had, 'a clear view of naked Jews, male and female, moving with a floating, unearthly slowness and a nightmare-like dignity among the clubs and kicks of the laughing German soldiers'.

Dodd's assured and flamboyant courtroom style was not to the liking of the more erudite lawyers present but his flair for drama undoubtedly gave the trial a boost. With both the damning content and sheer weight of the evidence presented by the Americans, the defense counsel could, at this stage, do little to aid their clients' cause. Their only comfort was that the prosecution team's performance was inconsistent – first scintillating and then leaden.

The presentation of evidence regarding the Nazis' spoliation of the occupied territories fell to the young lawyer,
Captain Sam Harris. Not in Jackson's class as an orator, he
began his speech with the words, 'My knees haven't knocked
so much since I asked my wonderful little wife to marry
me'. Guffaws rang round the courtroom and the British
alternate Judge, Norman Birkett, noted that 'the shocking
bad taste is really almost unbelievable'. Francis Biddle was
heard to mutter the more succinct 'Jesus!'. To his credit,
Harris recovered from this inauspicious start and Jackson,
mindful of the lawyer's subsequent career, had the words
stricken from the official record.

In the last week before Christmas, the trial turned to the
case against the organisations. Having earlier been
upbraided for the shortcomings of provision of documents
for the defense, Colonel Robert Storey presented the prosecution evidence against the 'Corps of Political leaders of
the Nazi Party'. The material was dry in comparison with
the revelations of the previous days and lacked the human
interest of a specific defendant in the dock. Storey did little
to aid his cause by returning to the tactic of wholesale presentation of documents to the tribunal. The judges' patience
was sorely tried by the increasingly repetitive nature of the
evidence. Lawrence, having forced Storey to concede that
one particular document 'might be considered strictly
cumulative', then replied, 'Well, if it's cumulative we don't
really want to hear it'. The defendants seized on this rare
opportunity to enjoy themselves and began to cheer every
fumble and interruption. Storey's less kind colleagues
dubbed him the 'Butcher of Nuremberg'.

His presentation of the case against the Reich Cabinet

fared little better before the Tribunal, as a growing impatience for the Christmas break made the judges increasingly tetchy. On the face of it, the case was promising because, with the exception of Schirach, Sauckel, Streicher, and Fritzsche, all the defendants had been members. However it transpired that the cabinet had not met after 1937 and that the Reich Cabinet had not been the agency by which the defendants committed their respective crimes.

The same problem afflicted the presentation against the SA. Although the 'Brownshirts', as they were known, were synonymous with the rise of the Nazis and notorious for their violence, the organisation's influence diminished rapidly after Ernst Röhm and much of the SA leadership was murdered in the 'Night of the Long Knives' in 1934.

Storey was replaced at the stand by Major Warren Farr for the prosecution case against the SS. Farr appeared no less ponderous than his predecessor, as he established the structure of the SS through copious documentary evidence. However, this proved to be necessary groundwork for putting in context the role of the SS in the running of the concentration camps, as well as the horrific activities of the SS Einsatzgruppen (or 'Death Squads') in Eastern Europe.

The case against the Gestapo and SD occupied the last two days of courtroom activity before the New Year break, which ran from 31 December 1945 until 2 January 1946. The New Year saw a welcome injection of drama into the American prosecution of the organisations, with the appearance of a series of extraordinary witnesses.

Otto Ohlendorf had come to light as a potential witness against Ernst Kaltenbrunner, the only defendant who was an SS official. Ohlendorf was an SS Lieutenant General, as well as Head of Department III of the RSHA (the state security service). Highly educated as both a lawyer and an economist, his dapper appearance and courteous manner made him the antithesis of the stereotypical SS thug. On the witness stand, he was helping to unwind the labyrinthine interconnections between the Gestapo and the SS when the American prosecutor, John Harlan Amen, astonished the court by turning to Ohlendorf's time as head of Einsatzgruppe D. Asked how many people this squad had killed under his command, Ohlendorf's dispassionate reply was that, 'In the year between June 1941 and June 1942 the Einsatz troops reported ninety thousand people liquidated'. He then calmly confirmed that this figure included women and children. The only humanitarian concern he had displayed during his period of command was when he had allowed his troops to dispense with the gas vans, because the removal of the tangled heaps of soiled corpses from the back of the vehicles imposed an unwarrantable emotional strain on them.

The appearance of so high-ranking a German officer as a prosecution witness galvanised the defense counsel into a vigorous cross-examination. The counsel for the SS, Ludwig Babel, seeking to limit the culpability of individual members, asked Ohlendorf if the order to murder civilians had been given a false veneer of legality when issued to the troops. Ohlendorf's reply chilled the blood:

'I do not understand your question; since the order was issued by the superior authorities, the question of illegality could not arise in the minds of these individuals, for they had sworn obedience to the people who had issued the orders.'

Throughout the proceedings, Francis Biddle had noticed a particular name cropping up from time to time. 'Who is he?' he had scribbled in the margin of his notes. The name was Adolf Eichmann. The next witness, Dieter Wisliceny, a friend and colleague of Eichmann, was able to satisfy Biddle's curiosity. Working as Eichmann's deputy, Wisliceny had been given the task of transporting Slovakian Jews to Auschwitz. When he requested verification of the order, Eichmann said he could show the order in writing if it would soothe Wisliceny's conscience. He then withdrew from his safe a letter from Heinrich Himmler to the chief of the SD, which stated that, 'the Führer has ordered the final solution of the Jewish question'. The American prosecutor asked Wisliceny if he had sought clarification of the term 'final solution'. According to him, Eichmann had defined it as 'the planned biological annihilation of the Jewish race in the Eastern Territories'. As to the scope of this annihilation, Wisliceny testified that, near the end of the war, Eichmann had told him that 'he would leap laughing into the grave, because the feeling that he had 5 million people on his conscience would be for him a source of extraordinary satisfaction'.

The last indicted organisation to appear in the prosecution's presentation was the German General Staff – High Command. This was a highly contentious case, as it had been vigorously argued that the organising body of the German military forces had merely executed the direct orders of Hitler. Moreover, it was claimed that, in comparison with the SS and the Gestapo, they had fought a relatively clean war. The American prosecutor, Telford Taylor, introduced as evidence the so-called Barbarossa order, a document regarding martial jurisdiction and procedure, which was issued by the defendant Keitel to German forces shortly before the invasion of Russia. Amongst its provisions was the directive that, 'Guerrillas should be disposed of ruthlessly by the military, whether they are fighting or in flight'.

To support his case, Taylor called to the stand Erich von dem Bach-Zelewski, who had been a General of the Waffen SS assigned to the Central Army Group on the Russian front, and warmly described by Hitler as the 'model partisan fighter'. To Biddle's eyes, Bach-Zelewski seemed like, 'a mild and rather serious accountant', a demeanour at odds with his brutal suppression of the Warsaw rising in 1944. Taylor drew from his witness the testimony that the Einsatzgruppen were pre-occupied with the annihilation of Jews, gypsies, and political commissars. Therefore the large-scale anti-partisan operations were not undertaken by vicious squads of SS fanatics but by 'ordinary' Army units.

Bach-Zelewski's appearance as a witness caused even greater furore amongst the defendants than Ohlendorf's. Jodl, Funk, and Göring were particularly incensed, with the latter calling him, 'the bloodiest murderer in the whole damn set-up'. Cross-examination of the witness by the defense counsel achieved little, but drew from him an insight into the mindset of the German people. Pressured by Rosenberg's defending counsel to give an explanation for the widespread barbarity, Bach–Zelewski finally responded. 'If for years, for decades,' he said, 'a doctrine is preached to the effect that the Slav race is an inferior race, and that Jews are not even human beings, then an explosion of this sort is inevitable'.

It remained for Telford Taylor to hammer his argument

home. 'The General Staff and High Command group planned and carried through manifold acts of aggression which turned Europe into a charnel house,' he claimed in his closing prosecution speech, 'and caused the Armed Forces to be used for foul practices, foully executed, of terror, pillage, and wholesale slaughter.'

Up to this point, the United States had largely held sway in the prosecution, as they carried out their case on the count of conspiracy. However, the British had managed to force their case on Count Two of the Indictment – Crimes against Peace – in amongst the American presentations. Sir Hartley Shawcross, Attorney General in Clement Atlee's post-war Labour government, made the opening speech on 4 December 1945. In the unenviable position of making the next opening speech after Robert Jackson's, Shawcross tackled head on the defence's assertion that aggressive war had not, prior to this trial, been designated a crime in international law. He contended that a series of international non-aggression treaties to which Germany had been a signatory, including the Geneva Protocol of 1925 and the Kellogg-Briand Pact of 1928, had had the effect of constituting aggressive war a criminal act. Accordingly, 'persons who, in violation of the law, plunge their own and other countries into an aggressive war should do so with a halter around their necks'.

A stumbling block in the path of Shawcross's forceful argument was the cynical non-aggression pact between Hitler and Stalin, made shortly before both Germany and Russia invaded Poland in 1939. Seeking to avoid the blushes of his Russian allies, Shawcross intended to portray them in his speech as honestly deceived by Hitler's false assurances of peace between their two countries. Getting wind of his intentions, the head of the Russian prosecution team, General Rudenko, insisted that Stalin knew all along of Hitler's duplicity, and that this slur on his leader's intelligence be deleted. As Robert Jackson noted, the Russians 'didn't mind being called knaves as long as they weren't called fools'. Shawcross duly made no mention in his speech of the Hitler-Stalin pact.

Shawcross went on to argue that the responsibility for the waging of aggressive war lay not just with Hitler, but with all the defendants. 'They are the men,' he claimed, 'whose support had built Hitler up into the position of power he occupied; these are the men whose initiative and planning often conceived and certainly made possible the acts of aggression done in Hitler's name; and these are the men who enabled Hitler to build up the Army, the Navy, the Air Force, the war economy, the political philosophy, by which these treacherous acts were carried out.'

Thus, in a lucidly argued, legally shrewd speech, Shawcross struck a massive blow to the defendants' hopes. Not only would their counsel have to take seriously the legal basis of the accusation of waging aggressive war, but also the charge would embroil many more in the dock than just Hitler's Foreign Minister, Joachim von Ribbentrop.

Shawcross returned to England shortly after his speech and the responsibility of leading the British prosecution case fell to Sir David Maxwell-Fyfe. In a clear, unfussy style, Maxwell-Fyfe presented documentary evidence of fifteen treaties, which Germany had signed and then broken. He was followed by four members of the British team who divided the case into geographical regions. Each element was simply presented. The relevant treaty was offered into evidence, followed by captured documents that laid out the military plan that had been drawn up to break that treaty. The invasions that followed were simply a matter of historical fact.

The whole British prosecution case was wrapped up in less than four days. Apart from the performance of the King's Counsel, Geoffrey Dorling 'Khaki' Roberts, whose presentation on the invasion of the Low Countries had been made in fruity Old Bailey style, the judges were impressed by the brevity and precision of the presentation. It provided a stark contrast to the more ponderous American prosecution case, which was taking place either side of it. This was partly down to the tightly managed focus of the British team, who had received expert briefs from the Foreign Office, and knew their material inside out. However, the British did enjoy the advantage of presenting a simpler case than the Americans. The former had only to present evidence that the men on trial were responsible for the crimes, whilst the latter had to prove that they had engaged in a common plan or conspiracy in order to carry them out. For example, Hjalmar Schacht had restored the German economy to a point that enabled the rearmament of Germany, but had he done so with the specific intention of enabling Hitler to wage aggressive war? Thus Maxwell-Fyfe could present his case on Count Two – Crimes against Peace – in less than four hours, while Sidney Alderman, who was the American prosecutor responsible for the wider brief under Count One – Conspiracy – required more than fifty hours.

On 8 January 1946, the American and British delegations began a presentation of the evidence against the individual defendants under Counts One and Two. That such a summary, which would normally take place at the end of the Prosecution case, was happening before the French and Russians had even started their presentations raised many eyebrows. It also revealed Jackson's underlying conviction that successful convictions on the charges of Conspiracy and Crimes against Peace were key to the success of the trial in establishing precedent in international law. Whilst affronted by the decision, neither the French nor the Soviets were in a position to start their presentations so could do little to stop it.

The case against the individual defendants inevitably repeated a great deal of evidence that had already been presented. Indeed Sauckel, Speer and Kaltenbrunner were excluded from the process, as it was felt that their guilt had already been sufficiently established. The British handled the cases against the soldiers (Keitel and Jodl), the sailors (Raeder and Dönitz), the diplomats (Ribbentrop, Neurath, and Papen) and Rudolf Hess, and Julius Streicher. Keitel and Jodl were dealt with simultaneously by 'Khaki' Roberts, who improved on his previous performance with a concise and pointed restatement of the evidence against the two defendants.

The case against Erich Raeder was presented by Major Elwyn Jones. As Grand Admiral and Commander-in-Chief of the German Navy until 1943, Raeder had played a crucial role in rebuilding the German Navy in the 1930s, and there was documentary evidence that he had urged Hitler to launch the invasion and occupation of Norway. Jones then presented evidence that Raeder had passed on the Commando Order in October 1942, which led to the

execution by a naval firing party of captured British commandos.

Harry Philimore had less success in tackling Karl Dönitz.
Succeeding Raeder as Commander-in Chief of the German
Navy only in 1943, Dönitz had been too junior an office to
have played a culpable role in the activities covered under
Counts One and Two. The British Admiralty, of the opinion
that the German Navy had fought a relatively clean war, had
been opposed to indicting him at all. Dönitz, however, was
an American prisoner, and had briefly acted as Chief of State
after Hitler's death in 1945.

Philimore was forced to focus his accusations against
Dönitz under Count Three – War Crimes. He called to the
stand two U-boat officers, who both asserted that Dönitz
had personally advocated murdering the survivors of sinking
ships. Dönitz's counsel, a serving naval lawyer called Otto
Kranzbuehler, carried out the first effective cross-examination of prosecution witnesses. He countered with the argument that Dönitz's order had been that, 'No attempt of any
kind must be made at rescuing members of ships sunk' and
soon forced the witnesses to admit that the direct murder of
survivors arose from loose interpretation of that order
under stressful combat situations. Kranzbuehler would
return during the Defence's presentation to further damage
the British case against Dönitz.

The evidence presented by Maxwell-Fyfe against Joachim
von Ribbentrop added little that had not already been
offered during the general presentations on Counts One and
Two. Proceedings moved swiftly on to the consideration of
the case against Constantin Freiherr von Neurath. Neurath
was a professional diplomat who displayed an unworldly

aristocratic hauteur. When first handed the formal summons in his cell, the presenting officer, Airey Neave, recalled that he replied, ' "I am much obliged to you, Major," as if I were delivering a Foreign Office Note, instead of a war crimes indictment.' He had been present at the Hossbach conference, when Hitler made clear his aggressive plans, and so was vulnerable to the Charge of Count One – Conspiracy. However, as a former Ambassador to both Rome and London, he was really only used by Hitler to present a veneer of respectability to foreign powers. After the invasion of Czechoslovakia in 1939, he was appointed Reich Protector of Bohemia and Moravia. In that role he dissolved the Czech parliament, took control of the press, closed down the universities, and implemented the Nuremberg race laws. Lampposts in many Czech towns began to display the notices: 'Reserved for Neurath'.

Franz von Papen exuded a similar air of detached bewilderment that he had ended up in the dock with common criminals. A career diplomat, he had served as a spy of legendary incompetence during the First World War. He entered politics after the war and, in an unlikely chain of events, was jockeyed into the position of German Chancellor in 1932. On hearing the news, the French ambassador in Berlin wrote, 'It was greeted at first with incredulous amazement. Everyone smiled. There is something about von Papen that prevents either his friends or his enemies from taking him entirely seriously'. Von Papen headed the group of conservatives who believed that Hitler could be controlled in their own interests and, as Chancellor, he introduced several laws favourable to the Nazis. He later served Hitler as Vice-Chancellor, and assisted him in the annexation of Austria. Beyond that act, he had done little to merit indictment, and the case against him was weak.

The evidence against Rudolf Hess necessarily had to pre-date 1941, but he was a central figure in the Nazi party from 1920, and rose to become Deputy Leader. From the documents he signed, and the meetings he attended, Lieutenant Colonel Mervyn Griffiths-Jones was able to produce evidence that he actively participated in the decisions and plans to invade Czechoslovakia, Poland, the Low Countries, and France.

Griffiths-Jones also presented the evidence against Julius Streicher, by far the least appetising of the defendants. This was not Streicher's first visit to the Nuremberg Palace of Justice. He had once visited a young male prisoner in his cell and horsewhipped him, for no other reason than his own gratification. The assessment of the Nuremberg psychiatrists was that 'this man is of a personality structure which borders on the frankly abnormal which bought him into difficulties even in the pathological social environment of the Third Reich'. The journalist, Rebecca West, described him less technically as 'a dirty old man of the sort that gives trouble in parks'.

Streicher was one of the earliest Nazis and one of the few men Hitler addressed using the personal 'Du'. He founded the explicitly anti-Semitic newspaper 'Der Stürmer' in 1923 and continued to edit it until 1945. The paper was widely distributed throughout parks, bus stops, offices and factories, and its relentless and hysterical Jew-baiting tone helped create the climate in which the Nuremberg race laws could be implemented. As objectionable as Streicher was, however, he held no public post after 1940, and had no direct involvement in activities indicted under Counts One and Two.

The American delegation presented the evidence against the remaining defendants, beginning with Göring. Being the most senior of the Nazis on trial, he had already been heavily implicated in the previous presentations, and nothing new was brought against him as an individual. The case against Alfred Rosenberg was presented by Walter Brudno, an oddity in the courtroom in that he had held the rank of Private in the US Army. Rosenberg himself was unusual among the defendants in that he was a Baltic German, born of an Estonian mother and Lithuanian father. Deputy leader of the Nazi Party until 1924, he was the most famous of Nazi philosophers and author of *The Myth of the Twentieth Century*. This hodgepodge of Nordic ramblings and pseudo-scientific mysticism was second only to *Mein Kampf* as the bible of Nazism, and sold over a million copies. However his fellow defendant von Schirach commented that Rosenberg 'sold more copies of a book no one ever read than any other author' and Joseph Goebbels had dismissed the work as an 'ideological belch'. More pertinent to the trial, he organised art-looting operations in France and other occupied countries, and from 1941 was Minister of the Eastern Territories. In the latter role, he complained to Hitler about the brutal treatment of Russian prisoners but, in time, was entirely circumvented by more ruthless and politically adept rivals.

Hans Frank was the leading Nazi jurist and was Hitler's personal lawyer in the hundreds of cases that were brought against him during his rise to power. When captured by the

Americans after the war, Frank handed over to them his forty-two volume leather-bound personal diary. Believing that the details in it of his complaints to Hitler about abuses of the legal system would help exonerate him, he was horrified to hear the American prosecutor, William Baldwin, presenting excerpts of it as evidence against him. As Governor-General of occupied Poland, he had stated, 'Before the German people suffer starvation, the occupied territories and their people shall be exposed to starvation. This means a six-fold increase over that of last year's contributions by Poland... It must be done cold-bloodedly and without pity'.

The most talented of the defendants was Hjalmar Schacht, a former President of the Reichsbank and Minister of Economics. He was responsible for ending the runaway hyper-inflation in the German economy and for constructing a system for obtaining foreign loans and credit, which made possible the massive Nazi programme of rearmament. Evidence was produced indicating that he knew of Hitler's aggressive aims, and was known to be in favour of them. However, the case against him was thin, since he had distanced himself from the Nazi regime after 1937. Moreover, he had been arrested after the attempt on Hitler's life in July 1944 and sent to Ravensbrück concentration camp. He was freed from captivity by Allied forces at the end of the war.

Schacht was succeeded in the post of Minister of Economics by Walther Funk. An alcoholic and hypochondriac, Funk was, by the time of the trial, suffering from diabetes and venereal disease. The chief of security at Nuremberg, Burton Andrus, described him as 'incapable of running a gas station'. A former journalist, Funk had coined the term 'Kristallnacht' for the attack on Jewish synagogues and businesses on the night of 9 November 1938. He became an important intermediary between the captains of German industry and Hitler and organised the secret funds flowing in to the Nazi party. As President of the Reichsbank during the war, he arranged for the gold teeth of murdered Jews to be paid into a false account, and the profits siphoned back to the SS. The case against him under Counts One and Two, however, was rather weak.

The prosecution found it similarly difficult to argue the case against Baldur von Schirach. His mother was an American whose ancestry included two signatories of the Declaration of Independence. Airey Neave found him 'perfumed and meretricious'. The prosecutor Dexel Sprecher argued that, as Head of the Hitler Youth, he imbued a warlike ethos into German children and that the Hitler Youth was a nursery for future members of the SS. This made little impression on the judges but, in his role as Gauleiter of Vienna, von Schirach had deported sixty thousand Jews to their deaths in the camps and ghettos of Poland. He boasted of this as 'an act contributing to European culture'.

Arthur Seyss-Inquart presented fewer problems to the prosecution. A former assistant to Hans Frank in Poland, he acted as Reich Commissioner of the occupied Netherlands from 1940 to 1945. In that role, he oversaw the seizure of five million Dutch workers for use as slave labour and the subjugation of the Dutch economy to the needs of the German people. He sent 117,000 of the population of 140,000 Dutch Jews to the extermination and concentration camps in Eastern Europe, his most famous victim being the thirteen-year-old Anne Frank.

The one defendant to be prosecuted 'in absentia' was Martin Bormann. He joined the Nazi party in 1925, and acted as private secretary to Rudolf Hess. After the latter's flight to Scotland in 1941, he manoeuvred himself into Hitler's inner circle and gradually established himself as the Führer's loyal right hand man. The most sinister and adept schemer of all the Nazis, he had a controlling hand in the policies concerning slave labour, the murder of the Jews, and the seizure of their property. His personal orders included an amnesty for German citizens who murdered downed Allied airmen, and the barring of the use of coffins when burying Soviet prisoners of war.

Wilhelm Frick was Minister of the Interior from 1933 to 1943, and was one of Hitler's closest advisers in the pre-war years. With a genius for pedantic bureaucracy, he oversaw the abolition of political parties and trade unions, and the internment of thousands of opponents to the Nazi regime. He used his legal training to draft and implement the Nuremberg race laws, and to allow the Gestapo totalitarian rule over the everyday lives of German citizens.

Perhaps the least distinguished of the defendants, Hans Fritzsche had been the Head of Radio Broadcasting in Joseph Goebbels' Reich Ministry of Propaganda. His own radio broadcasts eschewed the typical Nazi bombast, and attracted audiences in the millions. His reasoned, articulate style helped establish the cult of the Führer and to put a benign gloss on the increasing persecution of Jewish citizens. However, he was too junior to have any influence on Nazi policy and, as in the case against Julius Streicher, the prosecution laboured to establish that the dissemination of propaganda made him guilty of Conspiracy.

In total, these Anglo-American presentations of evidence against the individual defendants took eight days to present, and added little new evidence to what had been presented previously in the general submissions on Counts One and Two. However, the defendants now began to be more easily distinguished as individuals, and some idea of their relative culpability was established.

The French Case

The International Military Tribunal had been sitting for six weeks before Francois de Menthon rose to make the opening speech for the French delegation on 17 January 1946. Until now the French had kept a low profile at Nuremberg, and there was an air of nervous expectancy in the courtroom. After the ardent idealism of Robert Jackson and the urbane efficiency of Sir Hartley Shawcross, de Menthon would now speak for a nation that had directly suffered the horrors of the Nazi regime.

In a passionate but calm manner, he re-emphasised the jurisdiction of the court and the precedent of the 1928 Kellogg-Briand Pact in making the waging of aggressive war a crime under international law. His tone was extremely patriotic and his speech Gaullist in its sentiments. 'France, which was systematically plundered and ruined; France, so many of whose sons were tortured and murdered in the jails of the Gestapo or in concentration camps; France, which was subjected to the still more horrible grip of demoralisation and return to barbarism diabolically imposed by Nazi Germany, asks you, above all in the names of the heroic martyrs of the Resistance, who are among the greatest heroes of our national legend, that justice be done'.

The focus of de Menthon's speech was Count Three of the Indictment – War Crimes, which he divided into the categories of forced labour, economic looting, crimes against persons, and crimes against mankind. He ended with an appeal to the Tribunal, which echoed the optimism of Jackson's opening speech. If their judgement became a landmark in international law, 'the need for the justice of the martyred peoples will be satisfied and their suffering will not have been useless to the progress of mankind'.

The French delegation's case began with Edgar Faure presenting evidence on forced labour and economic looting. He announced that the evidence to be presented would relate to crimes committed, not only in France, but also in Denmark, Norway, Holland, Belgium and Luxembourg. This would exacerbate the problem of repetition that was already hampering the trial but would, nevertheless, give due acknowledgement to the suffering of these other countries (many of whom had felt underrepresented by the brisk British presentation).

The Nazi use of forced labour was contrary both to the Hague conventions and the Franco-German Armistice that had been signed in 1940. A slew of documents from the Nazi archives were produced to give some idea of the scale of the activity. By March 1943, nearly 250,000 civilians had been forced to construct the defences of the Atlantic Wall. Over 875,000 French labourers were deported to Germany. 150,000 Belgians and 430,000 Dutch were also forced to work in the cause of Nazi Germany.

The evidence given to support the charge of pillage was

even more astounding. Article 52 of the Hague conventions directed that an occupying army should acquire only the requisitions necessary for its own sustenance. The sum total of requisitions that Germany could legally demand of France in this respect was 74,000 million francs. By the end of the war, Germany had seized the equivalent of 745,000 million francs. From Holland alone, the spoliation included over 870,000 farm animals, 1 million bicycles, and 600,000 radios. The evidence for theft from Norway included 300,000 tons of hay and 13,000 tons of soap.

The French delegation then presented statistics to demonstrate the levels of starvation imposed on the populations of the occupied countries. Before the outbreak of war, the French average daily consumption was 3,000 calories per day. By the end of the war it had fallen to 900. The Dutch daily consumption fell to 400 calories a day. A report from the Faculty of Medicine in Paris concluded that 'it seemed that they (the Nazis) wished to organise the decline of the health of adolescents and adults'. A speech was offered into evidence in which Göring announced, 'if famine is to reign, it will not reign in Germany'.

On 24 January, Charles Dubost began the presentation on crimes against persons and crimes against mankind. He provided the court with a welcome relief from the onslaught of economic information by calling a series of witnesses, but what they had to say chilled the blood. Maurice Lampe had been an inmate at Mauthausen concentration camp. He testified to the fate of forty-seven captured British, American and Dutch airmen who were taken barefoot to the bottom of a quarry. 'At the bottom of the steps they loaded stone on the backs of these poor men,' Lampe said, 'and they had to carry them to the top. The first journey was made with stones weighing 25 to 30 kilos and was accompanied by blows. Then they were made to run down. For the second journey the stones were still heavier; and when the poor wretches sank under their burden, they were kicked and hit with a bludgeon, even stones were hurled at them. In the evening when I returned... the road which led to the camp was a bath of blood. I almost stepped on the lower jaw of a man. Twenty-one bodies were strewn along the road. Twenty-one had died on the first day. The twenty-six others died the following morning.'

Marie Claude Vaillant-Courturier was a member of the French Resistance who, in 1942, was sent to Auschwitz with 230 other Frenchwomen. 'All my life,' she testified, 'I will remember Annette Epaux. I saw her on a truck that was taking people to the gas chamber. She had her arms around another French woman. When the truck started she called to me, "Think of my little boy, if you ever get back to France". Then they began singing the "Marseillaise".' In a clumsy cross-examination, the defense counsel for Julius Streicher succeeded only in eliciting the damning information that, of the 230 women sent to Auschwitz in that convoy, there had been fewer than 50 survivors.

The witnesses proved the highpoint of the French case and, in contrast, the presentations on the enforced Germanisation of occupied populations and the looting of art which followed seemed rather pallid. The French were also running into difficulties with their presentation of documents. As with the American case, there were not enough copies of the documents. Moreover, the page numbering differed between the different language versions, which caused excessive misunderstanding and delay. Even the rather laboured delivery of Dubost was irritating the bench. An enraged Norman Birkett noted in his diary: 'There is no disposition to stop him and with complete murder in my heart I am compelled to sit in suffering silence, whilst the maddening, toneless, insipid, flat, depressing voice drones on in endless words which have quite lost all meaning'.

Birkett's suffering aside, the French case was, for the most part, skilfully presented. The limitations of the documentary approach that they encountered had afflicted the presentation by the much larger and better-resourced American team as well. Furthermore, the French thunder had largely been stolen by the Americans, who had already made detailed presentations on forced labour and the looting of art treasures as part of their case on Count One. It remained to be seen how much these problems would also affect the final delegation to make their presentation – the Soviets.

The Soviet Case

Roman Rudenko rose to make the opening speech for the Soviet presentation on the morning of 8 February. The courtroom was fuller than it had been during the French case, and this was largely due to the anticipation that crackled among the press. What mention would Rudenko make of the Nazi-Soviet pact and the invasions of Poland and Finland?

In his blunt and almost hectoring style, Rudenko and his Communist stance introduced a new vocabulary into the proceedings: the defendants were now 'Hitlerites' and the

Nazis in general 'fascist aggressors'. Going over the material already covered by the Americans and British, he touched on the invasions of Czechoslovakia, Poland, and Yugoslavia as preparatory moves against the Soviet Union itself. This was neatly done and avoided mentioning that the invasion of Poland was made possible because of the Nazi-Soviet non-aggression Pact. Göring and Hess had removed their head-phones by this stage in an explicit gesture of contempt.

Rudenko then turned to the crimes against humanity perpetrated by the Nazis. 'Having prepared and carried out the perfidious assault against the freedom-loving nations,' he said, 'fascist Germany turned the war into a system of mili-tarised banditry. The murder of war prisoners, extermina-tion of civilian populations, plunder of occupied territories, and other war crimes were committed as part of a totalitar-ian lightning war program projected by the fascists. In par-ticular the terrorism practiced by the fascists on the temporarily occupied Soviet territories reached fabulous proportions and was carried out with unspoken cruelty.' In a stirring finale, he called on the court to hear the Soviet case. 'In sacred memory of millions of innocent victims of the fascist terror, for the sake of the consolidation of peace throughout the world, for the sake of the future security of nations,' he claimed, 'we are presenting the defendants with a just and complete account which must be settled. This is an account on behalf of all mankind, an account backed by the will and conscience of all freedom-loving nations. May justice be done!'

The Deputy Chief Prosecutor, Colonel Pokrovsky then presented, in greater detail, material concerning the inva-sions of Czechoslovakia, Poland, and Yugoslavia. Since these invasions had already been covered by Sir David Maxwell-Fyfe under Count Two – Crimes against Peace – and by Sidney Alderman during the American presentation, Pokrovsky did little to advance the Prosecution case.

On 11 February, General Zorya began the presentation on the invasion of the Soviet Union itself. Announcing to court his wish to read from witness testimonies, he quoted the words of Jodl's deputy, General Warlimont, who was being held in the prison at Nuremberg. The judges allowed this on the condition that Warlimont be made available to the defence for cross-examination if they so wished. Undeterred by this minor setback, Zorya moved onto the testimony of Field Marshal Friedrich Paulus, the commander who had surrendered what remained of the German Sixth Army at the Battle of Stalingrad. Keitel's lawyer, Dr. Nelte, objected on the same grounds, arguing that Paulus would have to be available to the Defence, if the court wanted to accept his testimony as evidence. To the utter astonishment of everyone in the court, Zorya replied that this could be done by the end of the day.

Total uproar ensued, and Lawrence was forced to adjourn until the afternoon. The military men among the defendants were incensed. Paulus had been ordered by Hitler to fight to the last man, and was promoted to Field Marshal as an incentive (no German Field Marshal had ever let himself be taken by the enemy alive). To Hitler's absolute disgust, Paulus surrendered to the Russians, and even made anti-Hitler broadcasts for them during the rest of the war. The Soviets had smuggled Paulus into Nuremberg to testify without the other Allies having any idea that he was in the city.

The press gallery was packed to overflowing when Paulus was called to the stand as a witness for the Prosecution. Rudenko returned to conduct the questioning. Paulus's value lay not in his role at Stalingrad. He was able to testify that, when working for the Chief of the Army General Staff earlier in his career, he was ordered to draw up a full-scale plan for the invasion of the Soviet Union, thus giving credence to the Prosecution's argument that the invasion was pre-meditated. Paulus had evidently been well-prepared for his testimony in the Soviet style. Each short question from Rudenko caused him to answer effortlessly for ten minutes at a time without further prompting.

Paulus did not, in truth, provide any new evidence. But in the words of Telford Taylor, a member of the American delegation, 'it was fascinating to hear, from the lips of one of the few men who sowed the dragon's teeth from which developed the biggest and bloodiest war between two nations in human history, how and where the seeds were sown'. The following day, Paulus was subjected to a three-hour cross-examination by nine defence counsel. Under the barrage of questions, Paulus was not particularly impressive and often claimed ignorance of the facts or professed to have forgotten details. Göring scornfully quipped, 'He doesn't remember! Hess, do you know you've got a competitor?'

Pokrovsky then returned to begin presenting the evidence of war crimes against prisoners of war. Once again, the Nazis were damned by their own documents. An order from the German High Command to the Army in Russia stated that, 'all clemency or humaneness towards prisoners-of-war is strictly condemned. A German soldier must always make his prisoners feel his superiority'. The Chief of

Prisoners of War in Poland was ordered to construct open-air camps, and the accommodation for the prisoners was to have no roofs.

Much to the discomfiture of the other delegations, the Soviets insisted on offering into evidence the details of the Katyn massacre. In 1943, German troops had uncovered the bodies of thousands of murdered Polish army officers in the forest of Katyn near Smolensk. At the time, the Nazi regime sought to unsettle the Western Allies by accusing Russia of the crime. The Soviets in turn insisted that the massacre be added to the list of German war crimes at Nuremberg. Given the weight of evidence that had already been accumulated, the other delegations thought that adding this accusation would be needlessly risky. (Time would prove them right. Fifty-four years later, Mikhail Gorbachev finally confirmed the widespread belief that the 4,500 officers had been shot on the orders of Stalin.)

On 14 February, Chief Counsellor Smirnov presented evidence of the crimes committed against civilian populations. As the French had done, he included in his presentation the atrocities committed in other countries – in his instance, Yugoslavia, Poland, and Czechoslovakia. Once again the court reeled at the full horror of Nazi atrocities, which seemed to be even more savage than they had been in the West. As Smirnov argued, this was because the Nazi leadership had instilled in their troops the belief that the Slavs were subhuman, and that a reign of terror was required to subdue them.

The litany of horror was beginning to numb the minds of those present. An incident recalled by the journalist Maurice Fagence caught the atmosphere of alternate boredom and horror:

'[The prosecutor] was speaking about the murder of millions of men, women and children. The court yawned... We were thankful when the court rose and we filed to the Tribunal cafeteria to sup tea and talk sweet nothings. Presently a little Russian captain entered. We saw him pay 1/6d for his snack and put down his tray. Suddenly he plunged his head into his hands and began to sob. "Oh mother, sweet mother, dear father, why did they kill you?" Then, with understanding in our hearts, we went back to court'.

Smirnov turned on 19 February to the crimes committed in the extermination camps – Auschwitz, Majdanek, Chelmno, Treblinka, Sobibor, and Belzec. Captured German photographs of these camps were offered as evidence, and a film entitled 'The Atrocities by the German Fascist Invaders in the USSR' was shown to the court. Even those present who had seen the similar film during the American presentation were not prepared for the awful images presented to them. In the words of the historian John Tusa:

'It showed the warehouse at Majdanek where 800,000 pairs of shoes had been neatly stacked, the piles of skulls, broken bodies, mutilated corpses. There were sequences where naked women were driven to mass graves; they lay down and were shot; the guards smiled for the camera. The great bone crushers going to work on the 150,000 corpses in Blagorschine Forest. The women bending over corpses stiffened by cold, trying to identify their husbands and children, patting the dead shoulders.'

Judge Parker felt unwell and had to leave the courtroom. From this point on, all the judges on the bench seemed to interrupt the prosecutors and witnesses less and less. It became apparent that reaching a conclusion about the defendants' innocence or guilt was only one aspect of the trial. The other was to give voice to the suffering of the victims of Nazi Germany, to provide the stage for the cathartic act of bearing witness.

On 20 February, the prosecution turned to presenting evidence of the Nazi plunder and destruction of property. It came almost as light relief after the graphic horrors of the previous days, but the material was still harrowing. An order issued from the General Staff was quoted: 'It is urgently necessary that articles of clothing be acquired by means of forced levies on the population... enforced by every means possible. It is necessary above all to confiscate woollen and leather gloves, coats, vests, and scarves, padded vests and trousers, leather and felt boots'. The enforcement of this order during a Russian winter consigned hundreds of thousands of civilians to their deaths. Other forms of destruction were plainly wanton. On the estate of Leo Tolstoy, his books were used as firewood. When it was pointed out to the officer in charge that there was plenty of other materials to hand, he replied that he preferred the light of Russian literature.

All this material fell under the definition of war crimes, and it was not until 25 February that Smirnov turned to the specific charge of Count Four – Crimes against Humanity. These were not necessarily different to war crimes in either their scope or their horror, but they were defined as being aimed at specific national and religious groups. The most significant part of Smirnov's presentation was the evidence presented on the Nazi persecution of the Jews. The attempted extermination of the Jewish race, not yet commonly known as the Holocaust, had been given little attention during the French case (perhaps because the death camps lay within the geographical remit of the Soviets). Now Smirnov presented documentary evidence that had been captured from the Einsatzgruppen. However, it was the witnesses he called who made the most compelling impression on the court.

Severina Schmaglenskaya testified to the horrific treatment of infants at Auschwitz. Newborn children were separated from their mothers immediately and killed. Often this was done by hurling them into the furnaces of the crematorium alive. None of the defence counsel chose to cross-examine her. Samuel Rajzman had been an inmate at Treblinka, who had been spared death because of his language skills. He had witnessed the later arrival at the camp of his mother, sister, and two brothers. Workers who sorted through the family's clothes once they were killed were able to pass back to Samuel a photograph of his wife and child. The photograph was all that survived of Samuel Rajzman's family. Again, the defence declined to cross-examine.

A statement was read to the court that had been made by Jacob Vernik, also an inmate at Treblinka. 'Awake or asleep,' Vernik said, 'I see the terrible visions of thousands of people calling for help, begging for life and mercy. I have lost all my family, I have myself led them to death. I have myself built the death chambers in which they were murdered. I am afraid of everything. I fear that everything I have seen is written on my face. An old and broken life is a very heavy burden, but I must carry on and live to tell the world what German crimes and barbarism I saw'.

The case for the prosecution had lasted seventy-four

days, during which time thirty-three witnesses had been called and over two thousand documents presented. The performances by the prosecutors in the four national delegations had been something of a mixture; at different times dogged, ragged, impassioned, pragmatic, crude, and skilful. However, despite the occasional failing and administrative blunder, the prosecution's case had been hammered home, all too often by quoting the incriminating orders and statements of the defendants back at them. The defence had struggled with the unfamiliar system of cross-examination, but the trend was clear. Apart from Kranzbuehler, the defense counsel for Dönitz, not one of them had so much as dented the case against his client. It remained to be seen what evidence they could produce in reply.

The Trial: The Defence Cases

Göring

The news that filtered through to the cells in the Nuremberg prison on 6 March stirred the hopes of the defendants more than anything that had happened since the trial began. The day before Winston Churchill had made a speech, declaring that, 'From Stettin on the Baltic to Trieste on the Adriatic an iron curtain has descended across the continent. This is certainly not the liberated Europe we fought to build up. Nor is it one which contains the essentials of permanent peace'. Göring in particular was ecstatic over the thought of a growing rift between the Allies: 'What did I tell you? Last summer I couldn't even hope to live till autumn. And now, I'll probably live through winter, summer, and spring and many times over. Mark my word. They'll be fighting among themselves before sentence can be pronounced on us'.

It was, therefore, with an air of bullish optimism that Göring prepared to be the first defendant to be represented in the case for the defence. The prosecution realised that it was vital to win the case against him. For most of the period of the Third Reich, he was the second most powerful Nazi leader. He had played a key role in establishing the supremacy of the Nazi government in Germany, had been present at all the meetings in which Hitler planned his acts of war, commanded the Luftwaffe, and held overall wartime economic power as Commissioner Plenipotentiary for the Four-Year Plan. If the charges of conspiracy were to stand, a verdict of guilty against Göring would be vital.

The first witness to be called by Göring's counsel, Dr. Otto Stahmer, was a General in the Luftwaffe, Karl Bodenschatz. He had known Göring from his flying days in the First World War, and had later acted as a liaison officer between Göring and Hitler's headquarters. Bodenschatz testified that Göring had criticised the attacks on Jewish businesses and property during Kristallnacht, and had opposed war against Britain in 1939 and against the Soviet Union in 1941. The effect of this testimony was undermined by the fact that Bodenschatz had to read from a prepared script. He had been present in the same room as Hitler during the 4 July 1944 assassination attempt, and had still not recovered from the physical and mental scars inflicted by the bomb blast.

It was, therefore, something of a mismatch when Jackson began the witness cross-examination. That Göring had been angered by the destruction during Kristallnacht was not in dispute, but Jackson was able to point out that Göring had ordered the Jewish community to pay for the repairs, and pressured the insurance companies into not paying out on Jewish policies. Bodenschatz began to sweat profusely and became increasingly confused. When challenged about a meeting he had mentioned in his testimony, he confessed that he only knew about it because Dr. Stahmer had told him. This was by no means the toughest opponent Jackson could (or would) face, but the watching defence lawyers marvelled at how destructive the technique of cross-examination, alien to most of them, could be.

Göring's next witness for the defence was the State Secretary of the Reich Air Ministry, Erhard Milch. He had also been a close colleague of Albert Speer on the Central Planning Board, and was responsible for the allocation of resources and raw materials between the armed services. Milch contested that the Luftwaffe, which Göring had commanded, had been constructed for the purpose of defending Germany, and that any offensive role was secondary. He also repeated the argument that Göring had been opposed to war against the Soviet Union.

Jackson went after Milch with relish. The witness's position on the Central Planning Board meant that the same material that the prosecution had already presented against Speer and Sauckel could be used to undermine his testimony. When Milch insisted that he thought that all foreign workers in Germany were volunteers, Jackson produced evidence that Milch had been present at a meeting during which Sauckel had stated that only two hundred thousand of the four million foreign workers were there by choice. When Milch denied having a role in any war crimes, Jackson produced a document containing an order from Milch to hang Russian POWs who had attempted to escape. By the time he left the witness stand, Milch had done nothing to help Göring's cause, and little to help his own.

Field Marshal Albert Kesselring then took the stand, and repeated the claim that Göring's Luftwaffe was a defensive force. If this were accepted, it would weaken the prosecution's claim that Göring was guilty of planning to wage aggressive war. Conducting the cross-examination, Jackson asked Kesselring about the ratio of fighters to bombers in the Luftwaffe at the outbreak of war, and drew the admission that there were roughly equal numbers of both aircraft types. Kesselring also had to concede that the Luftwaffe was tasked with supporting the army's Blitzkrieg style of warfare, so that, while it lacked the long-range bombers present in both the British and American air forces, its purpose could still be explicitly offensive.

The last witness for Göring was a Swedish businessman, Birger Dahlerus. He had been active in the summer of 1939 in a bizarre one-man attempt to broker a deal that would avoid war between Germany and Britain. Dr. Stahmer had called him to testify that Göring had been willing to attend a meeting with Dahlerus and sympathetic British industrialists, and had arranged an audience for Dahlerus with Hitler. Why, Stahmer asked, would a man bent on aggressive war bother to take these steps?

Sir David Maxwell-Fyfe undertook the cross-examination of Dahlerus. He had acquired a copy of the book Dahlerus had written about his exploits, and cordially invited the witness to confirm some of its contents. In the book, Dahlerus had recalled his horrific realisation that, while the Nazis paid lip service to his efforts to negotiate peace, the invasion of Poland was already being planned. In his audience with Hitler, Dahlerus recounted, Göring showed his leader 'obsequious humility' while the Fuhrer himself ranted about exterminating the enemy. By the autumn of 1939, Göring was in 'some crazy state of intoxication' as he demanded that the Polish government surrender swathes of territory to Nazi rule. It hardly tested the forensic skills of the British barrister to make Dahlerus seem more like a witness for the prosecution than for the defence.

Göring had every reason to be dismayed by the course his defence had taken. The witnesses called on his behalf had done little to help his cause, and had been easily discredited by the prosecution. Despite the political rift that was apparently growing between the Allied powers, it was certain that, if the trial reached its conclusion, Göring would be found guilty. Unlike the other defendants, Göring was now not out to save his own neck, but to speak up for a defeated Germany and to conduct as passionate a defence of the Führer and the Third Reich as he could manage.

Two factors were now in Göring's favour. The first was the paradoxical advantage his own status within the Nazi regime supplied. While the prosecution was endeavouring to interpret events from outside, Göring had been at the centre of them. In addition, all the evidence was in German, giving Göring an instant understanding of documents, which the prosecution had to handle in translation. The second factor was the effect incarceration had had on him. The prison commandant, Burton Andrus, had arranged for Göring to be weaned off the paracodeine tablets to which he had been addicted. The prison diet and exercise regime had also caused his weight to drop from over eighteen stone to just over thirteen. All this meant that Göring's mind had sharpened and his mental agility had been restored. Yet, it was still possible for the prosecution to underestimate him. In the robust words of the historian John Tusa, 'It was still dangerously possible to assume that he was now nothing more than the self-indulgent, pleasure-seeking, drug-impregnated bag of lard with whom Hitler had lost patience and who had sat in Karinhall for two years painting his face and changing his jewellery'.

Göring entered the witness box on Wednesday, 13 March. His shaking hands and constant licking of his lips betrayed his nerves. Stahmer began to ask him a series of short questions and, as he answered, he began to relax. His answers grew longer and more fluent, leaving the court spellbound. Here was the most senior Nazi left alive, recounting graphically and without a hint of remorse, the part he played in the Nazi domination and devastation of Europe. As to the point made by his witnesses that he had opposed the war against the Soviet Union, he was keen to emphasise that his disagreement with Hitler was only on the matter of timing.

After Stahmer had finished his questions, the other defense counsel lined up to gather titbits from Göring, which would help the cause of their clients. Göring seemed happy to help his co-defendants but did little to spare their blushes. Ribbentrop and Rosenberg had no influence with the Führer, he claimed, because they didn't have his respect. Keitel's misfortune was that he 'came between the millstones of stronger personalities'. On the question of conspiracy he was adamant. 'There was no one who could even approach working as closely with the Führer,' he claimed, 'who was as essentially familiar with his thoughts and who had the same influence as I. Therefore at best only the Führer and I could have conspired. There is definitely no question of the others.'

Göring gave a bravura performance for over twelve hours of court time before Robert Jackson rose on 18 March to begin the cross-examination. It has to be borne in mind that, in the insular and feverish atmosphere of the trial, this contest took on a Manichean significance, encapsulating (in the words of the historian David Irving), 'the conflict between the ordered, civilised milieu of the wing-collared country lawyer, and the swaggering, arrogant, devil-may-care world of the big-time gangster in uniform'.

Jackson began circumspectly, asking open, almost rhetorical questions that sought to establish Göring as an unrivalled expert on Nazi matters. Jackson's strategy, as he later revealed, was to play on Göring's vanity, and give him enough rope to hang himself. But it broke the golden rule of cross-examination that you should never ask a question to which you did not already know the answer. Göring was able to respond at leisure and, by picking Jackson up on points of language and interpretation, began to dominate the exchange. Jackson tried to cut Göring's increasingly expansive answers short, but was reprimanded by Justice Lawrence, who said that the defendant could respond in whatever way he saw fit. Jackson was clearly irritated by the license given to Göring and grew increasingly flustered. By the end of the session, the prosecution had the uneasy feeling that their champion had come off the worse.

The following day Jackson resumed his questions, with an examination of the Nazi plans to wage aggressive war. He focussed in particular on the Rhineland, an area that, under the Treaty of Versailles, had to be kept clear of troops. Göring asserted that plans to re-militarise the Rhineland were not part of some long-term plot, but were cobbled together only a few weeks before the army moved in. Jackson then triumphantly produced a document, which referred to plans for 'preparation for liberation of the Rhine' nine months earlier than Göring had claimed. Göring calmly explained that the document had been mistranslated, and merely referred to a procedure for clearing the Rhine of civilian traffic should war occur. Evidently discomfited, Jackson pointed out that the plans were nevertheless kept secret. Göring replied, 'I do not think I can recall reading beforehand the publication of the mobilisation preparations of the United States'.

This rejoinder proved too much for Jackson and, barely in control of his temper, he appealed to the bench that 'this witness, it seems to me, is adopting, and has adopted, in the witness box and in the dock, an arrogant and contemptuous attitude towards the Tribunal which is giving him the trial which he never gave a living soul, nor dead ones either'. Lawrence attempted to calm the prosecutor but took care to repeat the earlier ruling that a witness could reply as he saw fit.

The cross-examination of Göring was at a turning point. Jackson had committed the cardinal sin in court of letting his emotions get the better of his intellect. Through press reports and radio broadcasts, news was spreading throughout Germany that good old 'Hermann' was besting the prosecution. There was a widespread feeling in the courtroom that the judges needed to act, both to save Jackson's face and to re-establish their control over the trial. No action, however, was taken.

The following day, Jackson again argued that the witness's responses should be curtailed. Lawrence agreed that Göring's remark about American mobilisation plans was uncalled for, but re-asserted the rights of the witness. Jackson then warned that the trial was beginning to get out of hand – a remark that could only be an implicit criticism of its handling by the judges. Lawrence's icy response was that the prosecution was under no obligation to tackle every irrelevant point made by a witness under cross-examination. It was a heavy hint that Jackson should drop the subject. Deaf to such advice, Jackson soldiered on, arguing that 'outside of this courtroom is a great social question of the revival of Nazism and that one of the purposes of the defendant Göring is to revive and perpetuate it by propaganda from this trial now in process'. This drew an immediate howl of protest from Stahmer, and Lawrence was in no mood to debate the issue. 'Mr. Justice Jackson', he announced, 'the Tribunal considers that the rule which it has laid down is the only possible rule.' 'I shall bow to the ruling, of course' was Jackson's sullen reply.

Jackson ended his cross-examination by turning to Göring's anti-Semitic views and, by quoting the Reichmarshal's own coarse words, was able to do some damage to Göring's stance as an urbane, if raffish, man of culture. Maxwell–Fyfe took over the cross-examination and immediately regained the initiative. With a far better grasp of his material than Jackson had shown, he was able to counter Göring's tactic of taking issue with small details in the evidence against him. During exchanges about British POWs who had been shot on recapture following their escape from Stalag Luft III, Göring became increasingly discomfited as he was subjected to a barrage of questions to which he could only answer 'yes' or 'no'.

Rudenko took over to question Göring on his part in the forced labour programme. In contrast to the wily approach of Maxwell-Fyfe, Rudenko chose to refer back to the evidence which had already be presented in the trial, and to harangue Göring into admitting his responsibility for those events. It was a brutal tactic, evocative of the Stalinist show trials, but it was effective in establishing that, because he held overall power in the wartime economies of both Germany and the occupied countries, there was blood on Göring's hands.

However, it was still Jackson's performance that set the tone. As the British judge noted in his diary, 'the trial is regarded as a spectacle, a kind of gladiatorial show, with the prominent Nazis like Göring taking the place of the wild beasts and prosecuting counsel as the gladiators and baiters'. In the glare of such attention, Jackson felt humiliated and was furious with the American judge Francis Biddle, whom he believed was using his influence over the other members of the bench to undermine him. Yet, for all the Chief Prosecutor's anguish, Göring's robust performance did little to dent the mass of evidence against him and would have little effect on the Tribunal's final determination of his innocence or guilt.

Hess

The defence of Rudolf Hess, in terms of both the character of the defendant and the courtroom drama, could not have provided a stronger contrast to Göring's. Since Hess's extraordinary outburst during the prosecution case, there had been unending speculation about his fitness to stand trial. He had apparently confided to the prison psychiatrist that he was unwilling to take the stand because of the potential embarrassment of lacking the mental ability to cope with cross-examination. His defense counsel, Alfred Seidl put a brave gloss on this decision and announced on 26 March that, because of his lack of belief in the competency of the court, Hess would not be appearing in his own defence.

Seidl's apparent strategy was to wage a campaign of distraction that would deflect rather than refute the charges made again his client. He announced that Hess would not recognise the Tribunal's authority to charge him on any grounds other than war crimes. As the ability to overrule challenges to its authority was written into the Tribunal's charter, it hardly mattered whether Hess agreed with the charges or not. He still had to face them. Seidl then stipulated that Hess was willing to accept responsibility for all his actions conducted within the sovereign state of Germany, and that therefore the defence presentation would not concern itself with domestic issues. This had the effect of concentrating the court's attention on Hess's involvement with Germans living in other countries. Seidl called as witness Ernst Bohle who, as leader of the Auslandorganisation (Foreign Organisation) of the Nazi party, had worked for Hess. He testified that Germans living abroad were never ordered by either Hess or Hitler to carry out any illegal acts in their countries of residence. Under cross-examination, however, the prosecution succeeded in demonstrating that the Auslandorganisation had acted as a fifth column in several countries, and was responsible for conveying military and economic intelligence to the Nazi regime.

Among the documents Seidl offered into evidence was a vast collection of damning verdicts on the legality of the Versailles treaty. This constituted an attempt to introduce into the trial the argument that the Second World War was a direct consequence of a punitive and iniquitous settlement forced on Germany in 1918. Maxwell-Fyfe challenged the relevance of this evidence, since the Versailles treaty played no part in the criminal charges that had been made against the defendants. Justice Lawrence asked Seidl if he truly believed that the treaty could excuse the waging of war by the Nazis and all the horrors that followed. Seidl could not answer satisfactorily, and the document was ruled inadmissible.

Hess's defence was thus soon over. The matter of his innocence or guilt had hardly been touched upon by Seidl's presentation, and the absence of the defendant from the witness stand meant that the prosecution had no real opportunity to advance their case. Since Hess had been in captivity since May 1941, the scope for finding him guilty of war crimes was necessarily limited. Yet Hess had joined the fledgling Nazi party in 1920, and had introduced the concept of *lebensraum* into Nazi ideology. He had been third in the Nazi hierarchy after Hitler and Göring. His guilt or innocence would largely be decided, therefore, by the attitude the bench took towards the charge of conspiracy and the importance they would accord to the pre-war crimes of the leading Nazis.

Von Ribbentrop

Joachim von Ribbentrop was the next defendant to have his case presented. As Hitler's Minister of Foreign Affairs, he had already been heavily implicated in many of the Prosecution's charges. He had, for example, provided most of the diplomatic overtures behind Nazi Germany's aggressive acquisitions of foreign territory. Few of his peers had any respect for him. 'A husk with no kernel and an empty façade for a mind', was von Papen's brutal assessment. Moreover, the strain of the trial had taken a terrible toll on his nerves, and his craven attacks of funk disgusted the other defendants.

Ribbentrop's counsel, Dr Martin Horn, repeated the tactic of Seidl, and tried to enter over three hundred and fifty documents into evidence. Most of these were untranslated, and often those that had been simply supported the 'tu quoque' line of argument which the Tribunal had already ruled inadmissible. With barely concealed impatience, the bench refused to accept over half of them.

Baron Gustav Steengracht von Moyland was the first witness. As State Secretary of the Foreign Ministry, he testified that Ribbentrop had often confided in him that Hitler had no use for a Foreign Minister. Ribbentrop had little influence on the Hitler-Himmler axis of power, he argued, and stayed in office only with the purpose of ameliorating the worst excesses of the regime. It hardly presented the vainglorious Ribbentrop in the most flattering light, but the 'noble intentions thwarted' argument was to prove a popular line of defence with other Nuremberg defendants.

In this context, it seemed bizarre that Horn then called Ribbentrop's personal secretary to the stand. Margarete Blank was asked by Horn to describe Ribbentrop's attitude to Hitler. 'To enjoy Hitler's confidence was his chief aim in life,' she replied. 'In carrying out the role set him by the Führer, Herr von Ribbentrop showed utter disregard for his own interests.' So effectively did she dismantle Steengracht's portrayal of Ribbentrop that the delighted prosecution declined to cross-examine her.

The final witness for Ribbentrop was Paul Schmidt, the Foreign Ministry's senior interpreter. He had attended Hitler and Ribbentrop during nearly all the major meetings with foreign diplomats throughout the 1930s. Under cross-examination by Maxwell-Fyfe, he confirmed the details of an affidavit he had made the previous November. In it he had stated that, 'The general objectives of the Nazi leadership were apparent from the start, namely, the domination of the European Continent, to be achieved, first, by the incorporation of all German-speaking groups in the Reich, and secondly, by territorial expansion under the slogan of "Lebensraum".

He went on to confirm that he had seen the majority of the defendants at the conferences where Hitler explicitly expounded these aims. Even if they had not voiced their total support, he argued, they had not raised any objections. Robert Jackson himself would have struggled to encapsulate the first two counts of the indictment (common plan or conspiracy and waging of aggressive war) so succinctly.

With his witnesses having done little but harm to his cause, Ribbentrop needed to make a dazzling impression on the court when he took the stand on 1 April. He failed miserably to do so. His rambling testimony included a diatribe about the Versailles Treaty, which was pointless in view of Seidl's earlier failure to have the issue recognised as a valid defence by the bench. A summary of all the hard work he had put into drawing up international treaties was met with Lawrence's tart response that he was in the dock precisely because the Nazis had unilaterally broken those treaties.

Under cross-examination, he was no match for Maxwell-Fyfe who had the added advantage of having presented much of the evidence against Ribbentrop during the prosecution case. On the subject of his honorary rank within the SS, Ribbentrop claimed that, because it had been conferred on him by Hitler, he had been unable to refuse it. Maxwell-Fyfe then presented the court with an application letter Ribbentrop had himself written to the SS, which included the information that his finger was a size seventeen should they be so kind as to send him a Death's-Head ring. The French prosecutor, Edgar Faure tackled Ribbentrop's assertion that he had not known about the atrocities committed against the Jews. So it was not true, Faure wondered, that he had demanded of Admiral Horthy, the regent of Hungary, that, 'the Jews were either to be exterminated or sent to concentration camps?' 'Not in those words,' he replied.

Keitel

General Field Marshal Wilhelm Keitel was outwardly a very different defendant to the former Foreign Minister. Whereas Ribbentrop was an ingratiating arriviste, Keitel had the proud bearing of the old Prussian officer class. Ribbentrop cut a pathetic figure; Keitel sat in court day after day with an upright pose and pressed uniform. Yet the two men had two things in common. The first was that they enjoyed little respect among their peers – Göring's description of Keitel as having 'a sergeant's mind inside a field marshal's body' was typical. The second was that both had been promoted to high station by Hitler because of their craven willingness to function as yes-men. The joke circulating Nuremberg was that the minute-takers at military conferences never recorded Keitel's first sentence as it was invariably the same as Hitler's last.

In the witness stand Keitel displayed remarkable frankness. In response to a question from his counsel Dr. Otto Nelte, about the atrocities committed in the Soviet Union, he replied, 'I bear the responsibility which arises from my position for all those things which resulted from these orders and which are connected with my name and signature'. What Keitel did deny was that his conscience should have dictated his response to the orders given to him: 'I could not say… that I had misgivings about questions of a purely political discretion, for I took the stand that a soldier has a right to have confidence in his state leadership, and accordingly he is obliged to do his duty and obey'.

Such moral bankruptcy was hardly forgivable, even when veiled in the martial ethos of obedience to superiors. But Keitel had not simply been an administrative cipher. Once he was aware of Hitler's views, he passed on orders with a passion and relish of his own. Perhaps the most damning example was the '*Nacht und Nebel*' decree, by which the Gestapo and SD were ordered to seize anyone considered a danger to the security of the Reich and make them disappear into 'Night and Fog'. Keitel not only issued the decree in his name but added his own view that, 'Effective and long lasting intimidation can only be achieved by capital punishment or by means which leave the population in the dark about the fate of the culprit'. Thousands of German citizens went to their deaths, and their relatives were never told about their whereabouts or what had happened to them.

Keitel's frank admission of his responsibility for the

crimes arising from the orders he promulgated made cross-examination almost superfluous. However, Rudenko and Maxwell-Fyfe were ruthless in their aim to establish his guilt. Again and again Keitel returned to his fundamental position, that he had ordered criminal acts without feeling that he was a criminal himself because, as a soldier, he was simply carrying out the orders of his commander. He grew visibly upset when discussing the Commando Order, which decreed the summary execution of any captured Special Forces. Maxwell-Fyfe hit at the core of Keitel's pride: 'What I want to understand is this. You were a field marshal, standing in the boots of Blücher, Gneisenau, and Moltke. How did you tolerate all these young men being murdered?' Keitel was the first defendant to admit on the stand that, while he could justify his actions in his own eyes, he acknowledged that the Tribunal could not excuse them. With the exception of Göring, who felt that he had bungled his defence, most people in the courtroom felt a greater respect for the proud but morally blinkered soldier as he returned to the dock.

Kaltenbrunner

In contrast to the prim and proper Keitel, Ernst Kaltenbrunner was a brutal hulk of a man who looked every inch a Nazi thug. Rebecca West likened his appearance to that of a 'vicious horse'. The prison psychiatrist had assessed him as 'a whining moral coward with an emotionally unstable, schizoid personality'. The strategy of his counsel, Kurt Kauffman, was to steal the prosecution's thunder and level the accusations at Kaltenbrunner himself, who then responded by evading or flatly denying every charge. He admitted that, as chief of the RSHA, he had been in charge of both the Gestapo and the SD. Yet he claimed that his own superior, Heinrich Himmler, had bypassed him and dealt with the head of the Gestapo directly. His own influence, he claimed, had been limited to the intelligence role of the SD.

During cross-examination, the American prosecutor John Harlan Amen produced a barrage of evidence to demonstrate Kaltenbrunner's guilt. Three witnesses had testified to seeing Kaltenbrunner at Mauthausen camp, laughing as he inspected a gas chamber and watching as different methods of execution were demonstrated to him. According to Kaltenbrunner, they had lied. A report which indicated that Kaltenbrunner had ordered the murder of a group of uniformed American agents could not be true, he claimed, as such behaviour would have been 'a crime against the laws of warfare'. Amen produced a signed letter from Kaltenbrunner to the Burgomaster of Vienna, cordially informing him that 12,000 Jews were being transported to the city to construct military defences. Kaltenbrunner insisted that he had not written any such letter and that his signature must have been forged.

Kaltenbrunner's chief witness was Rudolf Hoess, Commandant at Auschwitz from 1940 to 1943. He testified that Kaltenbrunner had never visited the camp, and that most orders that reached him during his time in charge had been signed by Heinrich Müller, the direct head of the Gestapo, rather than by Kaltenbrunner. Amen demolished this argument by forcing Hoess to concede that Müller had signed such orders only as a representative of the Chief of the RSHA, namely the defendant.

However, the legal point was practically lost amid the horror of the rest of Hoess' testimony. A meticulous administrator and perfectionist, Hoess was proud to tell the court how he had overseen the quantum leap in efficiency of Auschwitz as a death camp. He was flattered that Adolf Eichmann had credited him with the murder of two and a half million inmates. All this from a family man and animal lover, who would later claim in his memoirs, 'I am completely normal. Even while I was carrying out the task of extermination I lived a normal life'. For the judges who, during previous descriptions of Nazi barbarity, had begun to doubt that civilised men could possibly carry out such acts, Hoess was the definitive portrait of a dutiful and unrepentant cog in the Nazi machinery of death.

Rosenberg

If Hoess was an example of an unreflective executive in the Third Reich, Alfred Rosenberg was its foremost, albeit self-styled, intellectual. However much he wanted to turn every question put to him into a socio-historical treatise, Rosenberg had concrete charges to answer. He had acted as the intermediary between Hitler and the Norwegian politician, Vidkun Quisling, who urged the Nazi occupation of his country. As head of the looting operation, Einsatzstab Rosenberg, he had organised the seizure of artwork from its Jewish owners throughout the whole of occupied Europe. His rather feeble defense was that he had transported the items to Germany to protect them from damage in air raids.

However, the main prosecution charges against him were centred on his role as Minister of the Occupied Eastern

Territories. Rosenberg answered that he was only in charge of the civil administration, and that his powers in the Soviet Union were circumvented by those of Göring, as head of the Four Year Plan, and Sauckel, as Plenipotentiary for Allocation of Labour. Yet, under cross-examination, he was forced to admit that he himself had ordered that 'all inhabitants of the Occupied Eastern Territories are subject to the public liability for compulsory work'. In answer to his claim that he had opposed the worst atrocities carried out against the occupied populations, the Prosecution confronted him with the text of a speech he had made in 1941:

'The job of feeding the German people stands this year, without doubt, at the top of the list of Germany's claims on the East... We see absolutely no reason for any obligation on our part to feed also the Russian people with the products of that surplus-territory.'

Although Rosenberg's defence had become something of a hopeless cause, the court allowed him full license to express his philosophical views at length. A reporter for the Manchester Guardian described the mixture of boredom and irritation felt by those who heard him: 'For hours he [Rosenberg] maundered on. It was no more possible to grasp what he was saying than to seize a handful of cloud. Those who could went to get a coffee or an early lunch; others such as guards and messengers had to fall asleep.'

Frank and Frick

The one area of the Occupied Eastern Territories not under Rosenberg's control was the General-Government of Poland, which had been the jurisdiction of the next defendant, Hans Frank. A former storm trooper and defense counsel for Hitler, Frank had presided over a brutal regime in Poland. He had boasted to a newspaper journalist that if he were to put up a poster for every seven Poles shot, the paper and wood reserves of Poland would be exhausted. He had made a speech in 1943 in which he told those present that, 'We who have gathered here figure on Mr Roosevelt's list of war criminals. I have the honour of being Number One'.

The man in the courtroom at Nuremberg had, apparently, undergone a radical change of heart. He had spoken to the prison chaplain about his restored Catholic faith. On the witness stand, he made the most compelling admission of guilt yet heard. When asked by his counsel Seidl if he had participated in the annihilation of the Jews, he replied:

'I say "yes" and the reason why I say "yes" is because, having lived through the five months of this trial, and particularly after having heard the testimony of the witness Hoess, my conscience does not allow me to throw the responsibility solely on these minor people. I myself never installed an extermination camp for Jews, or promoted the existence of such camps, but if Adolf Hitler personally has laid that dreadful responsibility on his people, then it is mine too... A thousand years will pass and still this guilt of Germany will not have been erased.'

As refreshing as this sounded to a court that had begun to believe that the defendants were incapable of remorse, it is hard not to suspect a degree of slyness in Frank's words. His point that he had learnt so much from sitting through the trial seems a tacit claim that he was not aware of the atrocities at the time they were carried out. He neatly fingers

Hitler as the personal author of the policy against the Jews and, whilst he is happy to share responsibility, it is an onus he generously accepts on behalf of the entire German race.

Under cross-examination, Frank was keen to stress the limits of his own responsibility. Like Rosenberg he argued that his authority in Poland had been circumvented by Himmler's SS. When confronted by a passage from his own diaries, which stated his view that a group of professors at the University of Cracow should either be imprisoned or shot, he claimed that he had said that to misinform his rivals, and that he had in fact given the professors their freedom. This was the man who told his fellow defendants over lunch that, 'I think the judges are really impressed when one of us speaks from the heart and doesn't try to dodge the responsibility'.

Alongside Frank, the other prominent lawyer in the dock was Wilhelm Frick. As Minister of the Interior from 1933 to 1943, he had overseen the internment in concentration camps of tens of thousands of opponents to the Nazi regime by 1935. He provided the legal framework for the destruction of the rights of Jews within German society, and upheld the dictum that 'right is what benefits the German people, wrong is whatever harms them'. Frick's case was one of the fastest to be heard in the trial because, like Hess, he refused to take the stand himself. This may have been partly due to the fact that his defense counsel felt that there was little that the dry, unsympathetic bureaucrat could say to benefit his own case. However there was a strong suspicion that Frick's non-appearance was motivated by his desire to avoid questions about the secret funds he had hidden for the benefit of his wife and family.

Frick's counsel, Otto Pannebecker, presented what by now was becoming a familiar argument for the defence. His client had been pre-eminent within the Third Reich but, in reality, had wielded little authority. The true perpetrator of the crimes was the deceased Heinrich Himmler. Pannebecker called to the stand the defence witness Hans Bernd Gisevius, who testified that, indeed, both Himmler and Göring had supplanted the executive power of the Frick's Ministry of the Interior.

Gisevius' appearance provoked a far greater rumpus than his role in Frick's defence merited. A former member of the peacetime Gestapo, he had become an outspoken critic of the organisation once he became aware of its criminal activities. At the outbreak of the war, he transferred to German military intelligence and became the German Vice-Consul in Switzerland. From his post in Zurich, he acted as the secret contact between Allan Dulles, the Chief of the US Office of Strategic Services, and the anti-Hitler factions within the Wehrmacht. Evading capture after the assassination attempt on Hitler in July 1944, he had been brought to Nuremberg as a potential prosecution witness. He sat before the defendants as a living rebuke to Göring's witticism that the Third Reich was full of yes-men because the no-men were all six feet under.

The prospect of cross-examining such a sympathetic witness enticed Robert Jackson to return to the fray. Under questioning from Jackson, Gisevius admitted that legal responsibility for the Gestapo had lain with Frick until 1936, regardless of Himmler's machinations. Frick had signed the decree authorising the Röhm purge and put his name to the Nuremberg race laws. Gisevius then obligingly went after the other defendants. He argued that, contrary to the prevailing argument, Hitler had been greatly influenced by the likes of Jodl, Ribbentrop, and Funk. Keitel and Kaltenbrunner had far more power than they had acknowledged. Even the more detached defendants like von Papen and von Neurath had known of the crimes committed by the Gestapo and raised no objection. Several of Göring's skeletons were pulled out of the cupboard, as Gisevius recounted how the Reichsmarshall had been involved in framing and blackmailing anti-Nazi generals. By the end of Gisevius's account, Göring was roaring insults and had to be manhandled from the court.

Whatever Göring's feelings about Gisevius's testimony, two things were clear as the morally courageous intelligence officer left the witness stand. Firstly, despite his own lukewarm enthusiasm for the role of defence witness and despite the points Jackson had made during cross-examination, Gisevius had done Frick's case some good. He had been emphatic that Frick had been 'a minister with no personal executive power' and that he had had little contact with Hitler. Secondly, Gisevius's evidence had damaged some of Frick's co-defendants, particularly Göring, by contradicting their own accounts of events and responsibilities.

Streicher

If there was one defendant who would have benefited from imitating Frick and not speaking in his own defence, it was Julius Streicher. In the early days of Nazism, his rabble-rousing oratory had been second only to Hitler's. In the prison, even his most sympathetic fellow defendants were repelled by his penchant for exercising in the nude. Lurid rumours circulated about him drinking from the toilet bowl and his enthusiasm for displaying the proof of his nightly wet dreams.

Lewd and grotesque though Streicher was, his guilt was deceptively difficult to establish. The Prosecution's contention (as set out by the Americans in Count One of the Indictment) was that the Nazis had deliberately implemented the persecution of the Jews as a means of gaining control over Germany. Streicher's extreme anti-semitism had helped foster the psychological conditions in which theft of Jewish property and violence against their persons would be tolerated by German society. However, the British prosecutors had doubts about the strength of the conspiracy charge against Streicher, and preferred to direct their arguments towards establishing a link between the propaganda in his paper *Der Stürmer* and the atrocities committed against the Jews as encompassed by Count Four – Crimes Against Humanity. But even this approach was limited by the fact that Streicher had held no national role within the Third Reich, and that there was no documentary evidence to show that he had ever played an active and direct role in the persecution of the Jews.

Streicher began his defence inauspiciously by ranting about the inadequacy of his counsel. The hapless Hans Marx seemed happy to tender his resignation, but Lawrence sternly instructed him to continue. In response to Marx's questions, Streicher acknowledged that, as Gauleiter of Franconia, he had ordered the demolition of Nuremberg's principal synagogue, but he claimed that this was done to improve the view. (Under cross-examination he was tartly asked if the ninety-minute speech he had made prior to the destruction had been concerned with architecture.) He admitted paying four visits to Dachau concentration camp, but had done so to invite selected Franconian prisoners to a Christmas dinner. As to the organised extermination of the Jews, he claimed to have learnt of this only when in captivity in 1945.

Under cross-examination, Lieutenant-Colonel Griffiths-Jones read out examples of Streicher's writings. When describing the Jews as 'a nation of bloodsuckers and extortionists', was he not preaching racial hatred? Streicher replied that 'it is not preaching hatred; it is just a statement of fact'. In 1939, Streicher had written that there must be a 'punitive expedition against the Jews in Russia... they must be utterly exterminated'. In 1943, Streicher referred to Hitler's promise to 'free the world from its Jewish tormentors' and wrote, 'How wonderful it is to know that this great man and leader is following up this promise with practical action'. Yet under direct questioning from Griffiths-Jones, he still denied knowing of any organised killing of Jews. He acknowledged that he had been a regular reader of the wartime Swiss periodical *Israel Weekly*, but couldn't recall an article claiming the mass murder of Jews in the Ukraine.

As to the pornographic element of *Der Stürmer*'s antisemitic cartoons, Lawrence primly announced that they were no business of the present Tribunal. It was not mentioned at the time that Streicher's vast collection of pornography had been ransacked by American troops prior to the trial. Perhaps the most surprising element of Streicher's defence was the appearance of his wife as a witness. Many of the defendants had seen her at social functions sporting a garish diamond Swastika brooch. But there was still an almost audible gasp as an attractive blonde woman, at least twenty years younger than Streicher, took the stand. Adele Streicher gave a calm and graceful testimony that, for most of the war, her husband had worked on his farm and edited *Der Stürmer* without any contact with the Nazi leadership. As she passed the dock on her way out, head held high, Jodl remarked simply, 'Wondrous are the ways of love'.

Schacht and Funk

Hjalmar Schacht was, in appearance and ability, the antithesis of the abhorrent Streicher. He topped the list of defendants in the IQ tests administered by the prison psychiatrist, Gustav Gilbert, who described Schacht as possessing 'a brilliant mentality, capable of creative originality'. He had been interned in a concentration camp after the July 1944 attempt on Hitler's life and remained in captivity until the end of the war. He was astounded to find himself put on trial by his liberators, and openly contemptuous of most of his fellow defendants.

Schacht was an ardent nationalist, and was determined to help unshackle Germany from the imposition of the Versailles Treaty. He was the financial wizard of the Third Reich, arresting the economy's rampant inflation, and setting up a system of secretly funding Germany's massive rearmament programme. The charge levelled at him was that he had done this in the full knowledge that Hitler would use this military power to wage aggressive war. His defense was that it was his opposition to Hitler's expansionist aims that led to his disagreements with Göring, the nominal head of the Four-Year Plan (a scheme to make Germany industrially self-sufficient). Schacht resigned as Minister of Economics, was dismissed from his post as President of the Reichsbank and was replaced in both roles by his co-defendant, Walther Funk.

Schacht had been supported by the testimony provided by Hans Bernd Gisevius, the star defence witness for Wilhelm Frick. Gisevius confirmed that, to his knowledge, Schacht had only ever wanted to fund rearmament for Germany's self-defence. Indeed, Schacht had joined Gisevius on two secret trips to Switzerland to warn British authorities of Hitler's aggressive intentions towards Poland. Gisevius also offered a theory as to why so apparently prin-cipled a man remained in Hitler's government for so long: 'He undoubtedly entered the Hitler regime for patriotic reasons, and I would like to testify here that the moment his disappointment became obvious he decided for the same patriotic reasons to join the opposition'.

Like Streicher, Schacht's conviction was seen as a vital key to the success of the Prosecution's conspiracy charge. Without it, any further cases against German financiers and industrialists would be cast in doubt. For this reason, Robert Jackson chose to return to the limelight, after his ill-tem-pered and none-too-successful cross-examination of Göring. However, Jackson had not been closely involved in the preparation of the case and, like Göring, Schacht was a quick-witted and knowledgeable opponent. Jackson began by showing Schacht photographs of him with an array of senior Nazi figures. This was a rather clumsy ploy to suggest a greater degree of complicity between Schacht and these men than he had previously admitted. But Jackson ran into trouble when he asked about the chronology of the photographs, and Schacht airily made the point that there must exist a great many more photographs of him with all sorts of acquaintances.

Schacht was also challenged about his claim not to have been a member of the Nazi party. Why then, Jackson wondered, had he been in the habit of wearing the Nazi Party Golden Swastika? 'It was very convenient on railway journeys, and when ordering a car,' was the defendant's droll reply. Schacht, however, was less comfortable when obliged to admit that he had made donations of 1,000 marks a year to the Nazi Party between 1937 and 1942. Jackson then attacked Schacht's claim that the animosity between himself and Göring was based solely on their disagreement about the pace of German rearmament. To undermine this, Jackson produced a statement Schacht had made during an earlier interrogation:

'Whereas I have called Hitler an amoral type of person, I can regard Göring only as immoral and criminal. Endowed by nature with a certain geniality, which he managed to exploit for his own popularity, he was the most egocentric being imaginable... A lady who had tea with his second wife reported that he appeared in a sort of Roman toga and sandals studded with jewels, his fingers bedecked with innumerable jewelled rings and generally covered with ornaments, his face painted and his lips rouged.'

The courtroom rang with laughter, but Jackson had only established the rather mild point that Schacht was a hypocrite. Later that day Göring angrily denied the lipstick.

By this point Schacht was feeling sufficiently confident to answer Jackson's questions before they had been translated into German. He ran rings around Jackson on financial and economic matters. Once again, Jackson had broken the golden rule of cross-examination, which was only ever to ask questions to which you already knew the answer. Once again, he had ceded the initiative to the defendant, although this time without losing his temper. 'Nothing occurred during the cross-examination other than a strengthening of Schacht's defence', was Judge Birkett's pitiless opinion. For many members of the press present in the courtroom, it raised for the very first time the possibility of the trial producing an acquittal.

As Walther Funk had succeeded Schacht both as Minister of Economics and President of the Reichsbank, so he followed him in the witness stand. The talented pianist and *bon viveur* now cast a flabby and forlorn figure, resembling (according to one reporter) 'a gnome who has lost his last friend'. A former financial journalist, he lacked Schacht's intellect and ability. Moreover, by the time he came into office, Göring had control of the economies of the occupied territories and munitions production was in the hands of Speer. On the stand, he claimed, with some justification, that each of his roles had 'existed merely on paper'.

He was not entirely without influence. The morning after the Kristallnacht pogrom, he had proudly announced to Göring that a law he had drafted would 'Aryanise' Jewish business by barring Jews from operating retail or wholesale companies, keeping employees, or producing goods. In his defence, he claimed, 'We had to do this because otherwise Jewish property would have been free for everybody to loot'. Thomas Dodd, the cross-examiner, said that he must have been aware that the looting had been organised by the

Nazi party. 'Yes, most certainly,' he sobbed. 'That was when I should have left in 1938. Of that I am guilty.'

Dodd then asked, 'You were not ordinarily in the habit, in the Reichsbank, of accepting jewels, monocles, spectacles, watches, cigarette cases, pearls, diamonds, gold dentures, were you?' When Funk denied this, and claimed it would have been illegal to do so, Dodd ordered the lights to be lowered. A film was then shown to the court of the vaults of the Reichsbank. American troops opened bulging sacks bearing the Reichsbank logo, and heaps of the above mentioned personal items spilled out onto the floor. The Vice President of the Reichsbank, Emil Puhl, had provided an affidavit, stating that Funk had ordered him to accept deliveries of these objects from the SS in absolute secrecy, and not to ask any questions about their source. They were paid into a bank account under the fictional name of Max Heligel, which Funk had authorised. Funk denied this, denied knowledge of Reichsbank employees dealing with municipal pawnbrokers, and couldn't explain the provenance of the 12 million Reichsmark credits paid back to the SS. Puhl and another Reichsbank employee, Albert Thoms, were called to the stand. The two men and Funk proceeded to lay the responsibility for these deposits at each other's feet. One observer noted that 'the amount of perjury has been remarkable, even for Nuremberg'. It would be left to the judges to determine the guilt of Walther Funk.

Dönitz and Raeder

The case against the two naval defendants had been sufficiently dented during the Prosecution's presentation that it was likely that both Dönitz and Raeder could mount a strong defence. Dönitz's defence counsel, Otto Kranzbuehler, was a brilliant naval lawyer, and had already won the respect of the bench. Even before Dönitz's defence had begun, he had requested the Tribunal's permission to send a list of questions to Admiral Nimitz who, during the war, had been Commander in Chief of the American Naval Forces in the Pacific. The British prosecutors recognised that Kranzbuehler was seeking to put the German conduct of the submarine war in the context of American practice, and argued that this would fall under the inadmissible defence of 'tu quoque'. Kranzbuehler shrewdly argued that he wasn't claiming that the German navy's conduct could be excused by being shown to mirror that of the American submarine fleet. Rather, he wished to establish how Nimitz had interpreted the London Submarine Protocol of 1936. This law stipulated that submarines should not sink merchant ships without warning, and should allow their crews to abandon ship before the submarine opened fire. Kranzbuehler would argue on behalf of both Dönitz and Raeder that, at the outbreak of war, British merchantmen had both fought German U-boats, and reported their positions by radio. In doing these things, they forfeited their right to be classed as civilian craft. If the American submarines could be shown to have interpreted the role of merchant ships in the same way, then it could be argued that naval law had evolved during conflict, and the defendants could not be held to account.

No response had arrived from Admiral Nimitz by the time Dönitz's defence started on 8 May. Dealing with the charge under Count One of conspiring to wage aggressive war, Dönitz argued that he had held the rank of Captain at the outbreak of war. Therefore he had not attended any of the pre-war military conferences Hitler had held. Even at the time of the invasion of Norway, which had demanded far greater involvement from the navy than previous campaigns, Dönitz was still too junior an officer to be held responsible. Dönitz also denied the prosecution charge that he had ordered U-Boat commanders to murder the crew of sunken ships. He made the distinction between men who were still on board their ships, and technically still in combat, and men who were defenceless in the water once their ship had been sunk. 'Firing upon these men,' he claimed, 'is a matter concerned with the ethics of war, and should be rejected under all and any circumstances.' The U-Boat captain, produced by the Prosecution back in January who claimed to have received a fleet-wide order from Dönitz to do just that, was contemptuously dismissed by Dönitz as the only man who had interpreted the order in that way.

Under cross-examination, Maxwell-Fyfe asked Dönitz if he had passed on the notorious Commando order. He bluntly denied doing so, and attributed the murder of captured British commandos in 1943 to the local police, claiming that Himmler must have issued the order. But Maxwell-Fyfe made better progress with a memorandum Dönitz had written about 12,000 concentration camp prisoners being used as labour in naval dockyards. When asked by Maxwell-Fyfe if he had wanted German or foreign prisoners he replied that he hadn't given it any thought. The implication was that he had shown a similar lack of consideration towards compliance with the Hague Convention. Two days after Dönitz's defence closed, Kranzbuehler received his reply from Nimitz. The Admiral confirmed that, in operational areas, American submarines did sink enemy merchant ships without warning. With Dönitz and Raeder on trial for their lives, Kranzbuehler had struck a vital and artful blow in their defence.

In a quirk of chronology, Dönitz's predecessor, Erich Raeder, was heard next. He was unique among the defendants in that he had been a high-ranking officer before Hitler's rise to power. Thus, although Kranzbuehler had thrown doubt on his indictment under Count Three (War Crimes), Raeder still had to answer charges of waging aggressive war and of entering into the conspiracy to do so. In response to questions from his defense counsel, Dr. Walter Siemers, Raeder argued that he had been unaware of Hitler's aggressive intentions. In effect, he was claiming that, despite being present at a conference in November 1937 at which Hitler had discussed his plans to invade Czechoslovakia, Raeder had assumed that the Führer was bluffing.

Under cross-examination by Maxwell-Fyfe, he was forced to admit that he had personally urged Hitler to consider the invasion of Norway. Siemers hoped that the damage done to Raeder's case could be mitigated by drawing the court's attention to Britain's willingness to pre-empt a German invasion by sending an occupation force of her own. However, he lacked Kranzbuehler's cunning in phrasing his argument, and his request for British Admiralty documents was seen as an attempt to mount a 'tu quoque' defence, and thus refused. Maxwell-Fyfe also coaxed from Raeder the admission that he had passed on to the navy Hitler's Commando order. Unlike Dönitz, he could not

duck the charge through the denial of authority. The prosecution team had provided evidence of British commandos
being shot by a German naval firing squad in 1942, when
Raeder was the Commander in Chief.

Von Schirach

At thirty nine, Baldur Von Schirach was the youngest of the
defendants. Born into a cosmopolitan and well-connected
family (his grandfather had been a pall-bearer at Abraham
Lincoln's funeral), he had been charged under Counts One
and Four of the indictment. The prosecution had contended,
under the charge of conspiracy, that as head of the Hitler
Youth from 1933 to 1940, Schirach had trained Germany's
youth in the skills necessary for a nation of military aggressors. During the trial, Schirach explained to a prison guard
that the Hitler Youth were equivalent to the Boy Scouts in
America. The guard, who had seen combat against the young
defenders of the Reich, replied that he had never seen a Boy
Scout strip and re-assemble an automatic weapon in a
minute flat.

In the courtroom, Schirach's defense counsel Sauter
(who also represented Walther Funk) took pains to distance
the Hitler Youth from any military connotations. Uniforms
were worn, but this was to done to instil a sense of cama-
raderie and break down class distinctions. The Wehrmacht
may well have supplied the Hitler Youth with 10,000 rifles
but these were used only for competitive marksmanship.
Under cross-examination, Schirach made an uneasy impression. In the words of the historian John Tusa, he 'exuded the
whiff of the kind of scoutmaster who ends up in the Sunday

newspapers'. He struggled to provide an explanation for the letter he had written to Martin Bormann in which he referred to the longstanding training the SS had provided for the Hitler Youth. Although he claimed to have forbidden his young charges to sing militaristic songs, the official Hitler Youth songbook was shown to include lyrics like, 'We are the future soldiers' and 'Pope and Rabbi shall yield'.

Whether motivated by a desire to exonerate his beloved German youth, or to make a calculated pitch for the sympathy of the judges, Schirach did make an impassioned confession:

'I have educated this generation in faith and loyalty to Hitler. The Youth Organisation which I built up bore his name. I believed that I was serving a leader who would make our people and the youth of our country great and happy and free... I believed in this man, that is all I can say for my excuse and for the characterisation of my attitude. That is my own personal guilt. I was responsible for the youth of our country. I was placed in authority over the young people, and the guilt is mine alone.'

However damning this confession seemed, it was unlikely to be enough for the prosecution to win a successful conviction under the charge of conspiracy. Schirach had taken no active part in the planning of aggressive war and, apart from in social settings, he had had almost no contact with senior military or diplomatic figures. Members of the Hitler Youth may well have gone on to wage aggressive war and even commit war crimes, but no definitive evidence could be produced to prove that Schirach had incited them to do so.

Schirach's defence found it harder to answer accusations under Count Four – Crimes against Humanity. From 1940 to the end of the war, Schirach had been the Gauleiter of Vienna and had overseen the deportation from the city of 60,000 Jews. He had even joked that he would defend this action as 'an active contribution to European culture'. (Schirach was big on culture – he once declared that, 'Every boy who dies at the front is dying for Mozart'.) When asked if he was aware of their fate, Schirach did admit to knowing about the murder of the Jews. Again, Schirach was prepared to point the finger of blame at his Führer. 'That murder,' he said, 'was ordered by Adolf Hitler... his racial policy was a crime which led to disaster for five million Jews and for all Germans'.

Schirach's stance divided opinion amongst the other defendants. The less ardent Nazis like Schacht and Speer were impressed. Göring was so upset he didn't attend court. Hans Frank, whose defence had been based on a similar display of contrition, was reported to be jealous.

Sauckel

Fritz Sauckel was at the other end of the social spectrum to Schirach. As a former merchant seaman and factory worker, he was in the vanguard of Nazi administrators. He was appointed Gauleiter of Thuringia in 1927 and gained a reputation as a tough, no-nonsense operator. It was his experience with manpower issues that prompted Hitler and Speer to promote him to the position of Plenipotentiary-General for Labour Mobilisation in 1942. By the time Sauckel's defence case was held, he was close to being a nervous wreck. He had been charged on all four counts of the indictment, and his role in the appropriation and mistreatment of foreign workers had been heavily catalogued in both the American and French prosecution cases. When he began to give evidence, Lawrence was forced to interject, 'I do not know the German language, but it might make some sense for the defendant to pause at the end of the sentence rather than on every syllable'.

The basis of Sauckel's defence was that he had not wielded any real power. As Armaments Minister, Albert Speer told Sauckel how many workers he needed. Sauckel passed these demands on to local agencies, and it was the local Gauleiters who determined the living conditions of the workers who were seized. Unfortunately for Sauckel, it was known that he had summoned over 800 officials to a summit meeting in January 1943 at which he laid down the law:

'Where the voluntary method fails (and experience shows that it fails everywhere) compulsory service takes its place... This is the iron law for the Allocation of Labour for 1943. In a few weeks from now there must no longer be any occupied territory in which compulsory service for Germany is not the most natural thing in the world.'

One of the witnesses called in his defence duly testified that the real power lay with Speer and that Sauckel took orders from him. Another, a doctor at the massive Krupps site in Essen was called to testify to Sauckel's concern for the welfare of the workers there. However, in giving evidence, the doctor spoke of the rampant spread of tuberculosis and typhus among the workforce. After Allied bombing raids, the workers were housed in disused ovens and latrines. In refreshing the Tribunal's memory of the suffering the Nazis had inflicted on the populations of the occupied countries, it was hard to see how Sauckel's cause had been helped. None the less, Sauckel could not see himself as anything other than a decent patriot:

'I received a task and I received orders. As a German I had to carry out that task correctly for the sake of my people... As a human being and as a result of my upbringing I would never have supported a crime.'

The final judgement on his action would be made by the court.

Jodl

General Alfred Jodl had not been on the Allies' original list of war criminals, and there was some sympathy for him amongst military men on the Tribunal. It was felt that he had been added to the indictment largely as a symbol of the determination to hold the German army to account. Of slight build and strained appearance, he seemed to the historian Robert Conot 'like a man who had never smiled in his life, but had survived on a diet of bitter persimmons'. As Chief of the Operations Staff of the High Command of the Armed Forces, he had arguably had more day-to-day contact with Hitler than any of the other defendants. Although convinced of Hitler's genius for military planning, he was far less sycophantic than Wilhelm Keitel, and described the atmosphere of the Führer's headquarters as a 'cross between a cloister and a concentration camp'.

Jodl had been indicted on all four counts, and presented a robust defence against the charge of waging aggressive war. He argued that the re-militarisation of the Rhineland and the annexation of Austria did not lead to war, and so could be labelled as non-aggressive. According to Jodl, the attack on Czechoslovakia had not been planned but was in response to Czech aggression. Like Raeder, he maintained that Norway was occupied to deny Britain's own invasion plan. The neutrality of Belgium and Holland was 'really only pretended and deceptive' and Germany was simply fore-stalling any aggressive attacks by Britain and France. Jodl even argued that the invasion of the Soviet Union was in reaction to the mobilisation of Russian forces and was thus 'a purely preventive war'.

Given the weight of evidence presented by the British back in December, it seemed unlikely that the Tribunal would accept Jodl's explanation of German aggression. In explaining his own part in the planning, Jodl mirrored Keitel's defence that he had simply been following orders: 'As for the ethical code of action, I must say it was obedi-ence – for obedience is really the ethical basis of the military profession'. Yet he had perhaps unwittingly undermined the portrayal of himself as a simple soldier. Judge Birkett noted in his diary that 'Jodl gives the impression that he was much more than a mere soldier. He shows considerable political knowledge, much ingenuity and remarkable shrewdness'.

Under cross-examination, 'Khaki' Roberts was well placed to test Jodl's notoriously fragile temper. Prior to the outbreak of war against the Soviet Union, Hitler had ordered the so-called Commissar Order, in which he directed that the political leaders who accompanied Soviet troops should be executed whenever captured alive. Jodl had reviewed and drafted the order with the suggestion that it should only be used as a reprisal measure. Under aggres-sive questioning, this amendment hardly seemed to exoner-ate Jodl. Hitler also issued a Partisan Order which stated that resistance in occupied territory should not be punished 'by legal prosecution of the guilty, but by the occupation forces spreading such terror as is alone appropriate to eradicate every inclination to resist'. Despite the extensive evidence, presented during the Soviet case, of the enormous suffering this directive caused, Jodl remained emphatic:

'The principle of such warfare is an eye for an eye and a tooth for a tooth... I approve it as a justified measure conforming to international law.'

Jodl left the witness box convinced that he had proved himself an honest and honourable soldier. Göring and Dönitz commended his performance. Those of the defendants who didn't share his absolute obedience to their former leader were less impressed.

Seyss-Inquart

On 10 June 1946, the case for the defence of Arthur Seyss-Inquart was heard. A highly intelligent Austrian lawyer, he had been a passionate advocate of the union between Austria and Germany. As Minister of the Interior, he had worked with his fellow defendant von Papen, German ambassador to Austria at the time, to put pressure on the Austrian Chancellor to welcome annexation. After the invasion of Poland he went to work as deputy to another defendant, Hans Frank. In 1940, he was made Reich Commissioner of the Occupied Netherlands.

Like Jodl, Seyss-Inquart had been indicted on all four counts. Unlike the belligerent general, he was willing to accept responsibility for many of the charges made against him by the prosecution. He took satisfaction in administering Nazi rule in the Netherlands, as the population were regarded as true Aryans. He brought in Nazi supporters but also retained many Dutch civil servants. Yet he banned Dutch organisations down to the level of chess clubs, and arranged for any Dutchmen who 'violated the interests of the German occupying forces' to be tried in German courts. Hitler praised him as a model Reich Commissioner, 'a master in the art of alternating gingerbread with whippings, and of putting severe measures through with a light touch'.

The severest measures were directed against the Dutch Jews. He had intended to retain them in Dutch concentration camps, but Heydrich had ordered their removal to Auschwitz and other camps in Poland. Asked by his defense counsel if he objected to this decision, Seyss-Inquart replied, 'Since the evacuation was a fact, I considered it proper to concern myself with it to the extent that was possible for me as Reich Minister'. In 1943 he presented Dutch Jews in mixed marriages with the choice between Auschwitz and sterilisation.

The crux of Seyss-Inquart's defence was that it might have been much worse if he hadn't been in charge. He had negotiated down the number of hostages that Himmler had wanted to be shot, and arranged the collection of food for Dutch children. As the end of the war neared, he countermanded Hitler's scorched earth policy to avoid the destruction of Dutch property.

The judges would have to weigh these mitigating factors against the brutal realities of life in the Netherlands under Seyss-Inquart. He himself seemed resigned to his fate. On his way from the courtroom he remarked to Hans Fritzsche that, 'Whatever I say, my rope is being woven from Dutch hemp'.

Von Papen

Franz von Papen sat imperiously in the dock, looking like a European aristocrat out of Hollywood central casting. In reply to his counsel's request to provide a brief overview of his life and career, he began by saying that he had been 'born on soil which had been in the possession of my family for 900 years'. The strongest emotion he displayed was dismay at having been lumped together with the assorted brigands and nonentities in the dock with him.

Von Papen had been charged under the first two counts of the indictment, namely that he had aided both the rise to power of the Nazis and their preparation for 'wars of aggression and wars in violation of international treaties'. As a well-connected politician of the Catholic Centre Party group, he had been appointed Chancellor by President von Hindenburg in June 1932. However his repeal of the ban on the SA and unconstitutional appointment of himself as Reich Commissioner of Prussia angered von Hindenburg who sacked him six months later. Von Papen then entered secret negotiations with Hitler to create a new coalition government and, after Hitler's accession to the Chancellorship, he served as Vice-Chancellor for eighteen months. Narrowly escaping with his life during the Röhm purge, he resigned his position and became ambassador to Austria, in which role he helped engineer the Anschluss, or annexation of Austria by Germany.

Von Papen was not alone among the conservative establishment in miscalculating the extent to which they could manipulate Hitler for their own ends, but the Prosecution was hard-pressed to pin the label of criminal conspirator upon him. The case for the defence was not helped though by the repetitive nature of the material. The rise to power of the Nazis had been traced in great detail during the prosecution of Göring, and the Anschluss had just been covered in the defence case for Seyss-Inquart. To make matters worse, the laboured performance of von Papen's defense counsel, Egon Kubuschok, came in for swingeing criticism from Judge Birkett: 'He is not exactly to be described as a "windbag", because that implies some powers of rhetoric and possibly eloquence. Of these qualities this man is strikingly bereft'.

Conducting the cross-examination, Maxwell-Fyfe did his best to undermine von Papen's sang-froid. He quoted back to the defendant his statement given during interrogation that Hitler was the biggest crook he had ever seen in his life. In that context, Maxwell-Fyfe asked why he had written to Hitler after the Röhm purge in 1934 praising his actions as 'manly and humanly great' and 'courageous and firm'. Von Papen explained that he had genuinely thought at the time that Ernst Röhm had been plotting a coup. Given that one of von Papen's closest friends had been shot without trial and several of his staff placed in a concentration camp during the so-called Night of the Long Knives, it was stretching credibility to argue that he thought the Röhm purge justified.

The bodies did appear to pile up around von Papen. As ambassador to Austria, he provided smooth assurances that Hitler had played no part in the assassination of the Austrian Chancellor, Englebert Dollfuss. One of Papen's own assistants, Baron von Kettler, was found murdered in 1938. Why, Maxwell-Fyfe demanded to know, had von Papen persisted in working with the Nazis, if it was not out of sympathy with their policies? Von Papen's reply was telling:

'I did my duty – my duty to Germany if you wish to know. I can understand very well, Sir David, that after all these things we know today, after the millions of murders which have taken place, you consider the German people a nation of criminals, and that you cannot understand that this nation has its patriots as well. I did these things in order to serve my country, and I should like to add, Sir David, that up to the time of the Munich Agreement, and even up to the time of the Polish campaign, even the major powers tried, although they knew everything that was going on in Germany, to work with this Germany. Why do you wish to reproach a patriotic German with acting likewise?'

Speer

Albert Speer was one of the very few defendants who could claim to have had anything like a personal relationship with Hitler. This probably accounted for his indictment on all four counts, despite the fact that his active career only occupied the last three years of the war. Until then, Speer was notable for his architectural designs and his impressive staging of the Nazi Party rallies in the city in which he now stood trial. He worked for Fritz Todt, who held the rank of Reich Minister for Armaments and Munitions. When Todt was killed in an air crash in 1942, Hitler appointed Speer as his successor. Over the next three years, he steadily assumed control of labour allocation for the entire war economy, which at its peak accounted for 14 million workers in the Third Reich alone. The gravest charge he faced was the 'abuse and exploitation of human beings for forced labour in the conduct of aggressive war'.

Speer was certainly one of the best-prepared defendants. Since his capture his knowledge of the German war economy was in great demand among Allied strategists and the endless stream of interrogations taught him what the Allies most wanted to hear. He also extended his defence strategy beyond the particulars of his own case, by adopting a position directly opposed to that advocated by Göring. Göring wanted the defendants to present a united front. Speer, in contrast, encouraged the less ardent Nazis to recognise both the fallibility of Hitler and the extent of their own individual responsibility. Baldur von Schirach was one of the defendants most torn between the two philosophies, finally settling for the approach championed by Speer.

On taking the stand, Speer's defense counsel, Dr Fläschner, took him through the facts of how he managed his ministry. Speer reeled out reams of oft-repeated statistics in the manner, in John Tusa's words, 'of the confident young managing director reporting to his shareholders on the success of his firm'. Almost breezily he admitted that he knew that the majority of the workforce he employed was forced labour, but the responsibility for that lay with Fritz Sauckel. Speer merely requested workers, and how Sauckel procured them was 'no concern of mine'. In the same way, working conditions, however terrible they were, were not his responsibility.

Although it was not relevant to the charges he faced, Speer

was then directed by his defence counsel to explain his growing disagreement with Hitler about the outcome of the war. Speer obligingly reported that he had realised the war was lost by the end of 1944. He bombarded Hitler with memos to that effect, but to no avail. Speer was damning in his verdict:

'The sacrifices which were made on both sides after January 1945 were senseless. The dead of this period will be the accusers of the man responsible for the continuation of that fight, Adolf Hitler.'

Speer related how Hitler blamed the German people for losing the war, and believed that their loss should mirror his own. He ordered the wholesale destruction of German industry and agriculture, a scorched earth policy which Speer devoted his energies to thwarting.

Then came Speer's trump card. Would he care to relate, Fläschner enquired, his plan to assassinate the Führer? Speer teasingly demurred, and said it would probably be of no interest to the court. This was more than Lawrence could take and hurriedly he urged Speer to continue. According to his own account, Speer had been in a quandary. Should his loyalty lie with the man who had advanced his career or the country that man was doing so much to destroy? By January 1945, Hitler was conducting daily meetings in his Berlin bunker. Speer calculated that a canister of poison gas could be dropped down a ventilation shaft. However, on his next visit to the bunker, Speer noticed that an extension to the shaft had placed its entrance out of reach. The plan had to be put aside. The story had an electrifying effect on the other defendants. Schacht and Fritzsche were delighted, Frank and Jodl were appalled, and Göring fumed.

Robert Jackson returned to the fray to conduct the cross-examination of Speer. Courteously and gently, he encouraged Speer to expand on his view of the legality of his actions. Speer admitted that he 'did use and encouraged the use of forced labour from the concentration camps'. In response to the question of whether he had directed 100,000 Hungarian Jews to work in subterranean aircraft factories, he replied, 'In view of the war situation… I had no objection to them being brought to Germany against their will'. Like Seyss-Inquart, Speer felt that the provisions of the Hague Convention had been rendered obsolete by the demands of modern warfare. When asked about the appalling working conditions the conscripted labourers had to endure, Speer again trod a pragmatic line. He spoke of the 'universal human obligation when one hears of such conditions to try to alleviate them', but added, 'even if it is someone's else's responsibility'. Yet beneath the smooth words, a hint of the callous taskmaster shone through. When Jackson asked him to account for records of steel whips being used on workers, Speer thought it sufficient to explain that this must have been due to a shortage of rubber with which to make truncheons.

At the end of the cross-examination, Jackson tried to pin Speer down on the notion of responsibility. As a member of the government, he accepted responsibility for the large policies, but not for all the details that occurred in their execution: 'The leaders must accept a common responsibility … after the catastrophe, for if the war had been won the leaders would also have presumably laid claim to common responsibility. But to what extent that is punishable under law or ethics I cannot decide, and it was not my purpose to decide.'

Von Neurath and Fritzsche

After Speer, the appearance of Konstantin von Neurath on the witness stand was an inevitable anti-climax. At seventy-four, he was the oldest defendant and, like von Papen, attempted to remain as aristocratically aloof from the proceedings as possible. His defense counsel, von Lüdinghausen, made much of his client's lineage, and the rambling account of how Neurath's grandfather, great-grandfather and great-great-grandfather had all been selfless public servants attracted regular interruptions from the bench. Time and again Lawrence pointed out that the indictment only concerned von Neurath's career, from the time he entered von Papen's cabinet as Foreign Minister in 1932. He continued in that role when Hitler came to power, until he resigned in 1938 and was replaced by von Ribbentrop. In response to his counsel's questions, von Neurath claimed that he tendered his resignation upon discovering Hitler's aggressive intentions. However this apparently high-minded stance was undercut by the fact that he continued to hold the rank of Reich Minister, and was diplomatically active during the Anschluss, even promising the Czechs that the Führer held no aggressive intentions towards them. Whilst not necessarily at the centre of Hitler's coterie, he provided his regime with a reassuring, patrician gloss.

Von Neurath also faced charges arising from his role as Reich Protector of Bohemia and Moravia. He claimed that he had been given this role precisely because Hitler wanted moderate and restrained government of the region. Whilst not in the same brutal league as his co-defendant Hans Frank, von Neurath nevertheless oversaw the introduction of the Nuremberg Laws, the shackling of the local economy to the demands of the Reich, and the round-up of forced labour. Like many of his colleagues he sought to limit his own responsibility for these actions by claiming that it was Heinrich Himmler who wielded the real power behind the throne.

Conducting the cross-examination, Maxwell-Fyfe attacked von Neurath's moral stance, quoting from a letter the defendant had written in 1940, suggesting that, in Bohemia and Moravia, the regime should keep 'those suitable for Germanisation by individual selective breeding... while expelling those who are not useful from a racial standpoint and are enemies of the Reich'. Von Neurath was clearly flustered by this attack, but clung to his defence that he had remained in power to exercise a moderating influence. 'Did you ever hear that every cabinet minister must leave the cabinet if he does not agree with one particular thing?' he asked. Maxwell-Fyfe's reply was withering: 'Yes, every cabinet minister for whom I have any respect left a cabinet if it did something of which he morally disapproved'.

Von Neurath's case was then followed by that of the last defendant in the dock, Hans Fritzsche. Although indicted on Counts One, Three, and Four, he was the lowest ranking Nazi on trial, and there was a healthy suspicion amongst many present that the case against him had been hastily cobbled together, because the suicide of Joseph Goebbels had deprived the court of the chance to try the leading propagandist in the Third Reich. The Prosecution claimed that Fritzsche's popular radio broadcasts had helped win the German people over to the aggressive aims of the Nazis.

However, the charge that this denoted an active role in the criminal conspiracy was undermined by the fact that Fritzsche had never met Hitler and had met only four of his fellow defendants prior to his capture at the end of the war. In his defense, Fritzsche claimed that at the time he had been as much duped as anyone by the propaganda he had been ordered to broadcast.

The prosecution case was on more solid ground on Counts Three and Four in accusing Fritzsche of inciting crimes against the populations of the occupied territories. Broadcasting on the advance by German troops into Soviet territory he claimed that, 'in this struggle in the East... culture, civilisation, and human decency make a stand against the diabolical principle of a subhuman world'. Acknowledging his own anti-semitism, he admitted that he had wanted 'a restriction on the predominant influence of Jewry in German politics, economy, and culture'. However, as with the case against Julius Streicher, there was a crucial legal distinction between identifying an individual's deplorable statements and proving that such statements directly caused others to commit crimes. Propaganda per se was not a crime on the indictment.

Fritzsche had sat through enough of the trial to know what went down well with the judges. In the face of crude cross-examination by the Soviet prosecutor, Fritzsche was at pains to focus the blame for atrocities on the Nazi leadership;

'If the German people had learned of these mass murders, they would certainly have no longer supported Hitler. They would probably have sacrificed five million for a victory, but never would the German people have wished to bring about victory by the murder of five million people.'

Bormann

With the benefit of hindsight the decision to try Martin Bormann, absent and in all likelihood dead, seems a curious one. Yet, at the time, it was not so obvious that Hitler's private secretary and right-hand man was beyond the reach of justice. Conflicting evidence from those who had witnessed Bormann's flight from Hitler's bunker on 1 May 1945 left open the possibility that he had survived. In the circumstances, Maxwell Fyfe for the Prosecution argued that Bormann came within the remit of the court as defined by the words of the Charter: 'The Tribunal shall have the right to take proceedings against a person charged with crimes set out in Article 6 of this Charter in his absence, if he has not been found'. In the event, Bormann was found guilty on two of the four counts and the judges, declaring that the evidence of his death was not conclusive, sentenced him to death *in absentia*. A proviso was added to the judgement stating that, if he should be found, the fact that he had not been present for his trial would be taken into account and, if there was any mitigating evidence forthcoming, his sentence might be altered or reduced.

The Trial Concludes

Closing Speeches

It had been intended that the defence for the indicted organisations would follow. However, the summoning of witnesses for those cases was not complete and, rather than stall proceedings, the Tribunal decided that the closing arguments from the counsels for the defendants be heard immediately. The judges were at pains to prevent unnecessary repetition and time wasting by limiting each lawyer to half a day of court time and by insisting that a printed copy of each speech be handed over in advance. By these means the judges were able to take a blue pencil to the passage in the speech of Kaltenbrunner's counsel, in which he proposed to discuss 'Renaissance, Subjectivism, the French Revolution and National Socialism'. Even so, Lawrence was obliged to reprimand him mid-speech:

'Is it not time that you came to the case of the defendant that you represent? The tribunal proposes, as far as it can, to decide the cases which it has to decide in accordance with law and not with the sort of very general, very vague and misty philosophical doctrine with which you appear to be dealing.'

Without contributions from the defendants themselves,

press interest dwindled and, in the words of the journalist Rebecca West, the courtroom became a 'citadel of boredom'. However, without the demands of cross-examination, many of the defence lawyers became more composed and, within their speeches and an opening presentation by Dr. Jahreiss, the key arguments were eloquently presented.

The first was that the trial was being conducted in circumstances that ruled out the possibility of an impartial verdict. The judges were drawn from the victorious powers and the defendants from the vanquished. It was a recipe for vengeance and not justice. The second was that the trial was founded on new law. In the case of waging aggressive war, the defence contended that the Kellogg-Briand Pact had condemned it but not outlawed it. Thus when the Charter of the International Military Tribunal defined aggressive war as illegal, they were holding the defendants responsible for acts that had not technically been crimes when they had committed them. Moreover, it was contested, current international law made no provision for holding individuals responsible for acts committed by the state. It was as if the Tribunal was drafting law with the specific intention of establishing the guilt of the men on trial.

The third argument was that the leadership system (or *Führerprinzip*) of the Third Reich resulted in all orders emanating from Adolf Hitler. However senior in the Party hierarchy the defendants seemed, they were all honour bound to follow the orders of their leader without question. One of the defence lawyers, Dix, went as far as to suggest that the obedience shown to Hitler by the defendants was 'the quiet of the churchyard enforced through terror'. Whatever the motivation, the defence argued, the responsibility for the crimes perpetrated in the name of the Third Reich lay with its deceased leader.

Robert Jackson returned to the stand to make the first closing speech for the prosecution. Still bridling from reaction to his cross-examinations of Göring and Speer, he quickly hit the rhetorical heights of his opening speech so many months earlier.

'In eight months we have introduced evidence which embraces as vast and varied a panorama of events as has ever been compressed within the framework of a litigation. It is impossible in summation to do more than outline with bold strokes the vitals of this trial's mad and melancholy record.'

He was dismissive of the defence's arguments about the legitimacy of the trial, quoting the dictum that, 'No thief 'ere felt the halter draw with good opinion of the law'. Indeed the victorious Allies had given the defendants 'the kind of trial which they, in the days of their pomp and power, never gave to any man'.

However, in the pen portraits that followed, Jackson was keen to emphasise the roles played by those defendants against whom the prosecution had mounted the weakest cases. Von Papen was styled the 'pious agent of an infidel regime' who 'held the stirrups while Hitler vaulted into the saddle'. Von Neurath was the 'old school diplomat, who cast the pearls of his experience before Nazis' while Schacht offered them a 'façade of starched respectability'.

As to the claim that *Führerprinzip* absolved the defendants of responsibility for their actions, Jackson was dogmatic.

'I admit that Hitler was the chief villain. But for the defendants to put all blame on him is neither manly nor true. Other legs must run his errands; other hands must execute his plans. On whom did Hitler rely on such things more than upon these men in the dock?'

Sir Hartley Shawcross returned to Nuremberg to deliver the closing address for the British delegation. Less orotund than Jackson, he was held in high regard even by the defendants, but gave them no respite. He listed every act of aggression by Nazi Germany up to and including the invasion of the Soviet Union in 1941:

'In no single case did a declaration of war precede military action... In every single case, as the documents made clear, that was the common plan... Every one of these men acquiesced in this technique, knowing full well what it must represent in terms of human life. How can any one of them now say he was not party to common murder in its most ruthless form?'

To reinforce the charge that the defendants were murderers, Shawcross also read from a harrowing affidavit by Hermann Gräbe, a German construction manager who worked for the Wehrmacht in occupied Ukraine. Despite the months of gruesome evidence that had preceded this moment, Gräbe's account of a massacre of local Jews left the court in horrified silence:

'During the fifteen minutes that I stood near the pit I heard no complaint or plea for mercy. I watched a family of about 8 persons, a man and a woman, both about fifty with their children of about 1, 8 and 10, and two grown-up daughters of about twenty to twenty-four. An old woman with snow-white hair was holding the one-year old child in her arms and singing to it, and tickling it. The child was cooing with delight. The couple were looking on with tears in their eyes. The father was holding the hand of a boy about 10 years old and speaking to him softly; the boy was fighting his tears. The father pointed towards the sky, stroked his head, and seemed to explain something to him.'

According to Rebecca West, at this point, 'all the defendants wriggled on their seats, like children rated by a schoolmaster, while their faces grew old'.

Shawcross concluded with a demand that the people ultimately responsible for such tragedies should be held to account. The defendants themselves were no longer in positions of authority – 'their personal power for evil lies forever broken' – but it was important that they should pay for what they had done in the past. In a sense, their individual fates were insignificant but 'the ways of truth and righteousness between the nations of the world, the hope of future international co-operation in the administration of law and justice' depended on the sentences meted out by the Tribunal.

Both Jackson and Shawcross had delivered such powerful and moving speeches that the final addresses of Dubost and Rudenko, the French and Russian counsels, seemed anti-climactic. They were able only to reiterate what the American and British prosecutors had already said but, between them, the four men had presented a telling and appalling indictment of Nazi crimes.

After the closing arguments by both the defence and the prosecution, it was finally time to hear the defence cases for the indicted organisations. The Charter of the Indictment had granted the right of appeal to members of the organisations, and this right had been communicated through newspapers, broadcasts, and fliers in October the previous year.

By the beginning of April 1946, over 47,000 applications had been lodged. This was testimony to the fear that the trial had aroused in the German people: if the organisations were found guilty, then hundreds of thousands of Germans could be declared criminals at a stroke. Jackson was at pains to re-assure the populace by declaring that 'the United States is not interested in coming over here 3,500 miles to prosecute clerks and stenographers and janitors,' but the definitions of membership and culpability remained thorny issues throughout the presentation of the defence's case.

The first case, heard over the last two days of July, was that of the Corps of the Political Leaders of the Nazi Party. The posts at the top of the Corps' hierarchy, the Reichs-leiters and Gauleiters, had representatives already in the dock. However, the counsel for the defence, Robert Servatius, was successful in establishing that, at the lowest tier of the structure, the Blockleiters, many were co-opted into the role and the posts were poorly paid and often part-time. It was hard to see how men concerned with collecting local revenue for the Nazi party and organising assistance after air raids were engaged in the vast criminal conspiracy to wage aggressive war. Moreover, as distasteful as they may have been, organising support for Hitler, participation in the disbandment of trade unions, and complicity in the violence of Kristallnacht, were not war crimes.

Rudolf Merkel, who was defending the Gestapo (the Secret State Police) and the SD (the Security Service of the SS), also adopted the tactic of stressing the non-executive and administrative roles within an organisation. No matter the number of typists and telephone operators, however, an enormous body of evidence had already been entered into the trial's record as to the role of both organisations in the arrest, torture and execution of political opponents, hostages and captured Allied combatants. The witnesses who appeared on the stand were swiftly reduced to claiming their own personal innocence and pointing the blame at the SS.

The defence case for the SS took six days to hear. Like the Gestapo, the reputation of the SS had been more than blackened by previous testimony, not least that of Otto Ohlendorf. It was argued that the SS was, in reality, a vast empire of independent units that knew little of what the wider organisation was doing. Thus criminal responsibility lay only with the overall head, Heinrich Himmler. The witnesses who were heard hardly supported this contention.

Wolfram Sievers of the Ancestral Heritage Society had employed the SS to procure the skulls of Jewish-Bolshevik political commissars for his anthropological research. Under cross-examination by the Prosecution, he was forced to reveal details of medical experiments SS doctors had carried out for the Luftwaffe. Even by the standards of the previous months, the details of the suffering imposed on concentration camp inmates were revolting.

There was a moment of black comedy amid the horror when an SS judge was recounting the excellent facilities he had observed at the Buchenwald concentration camp. As well as a library and a cinema, he claimed that prisoners had access to a brothel. Momentarily lulled into sleep by the summer heat in the courtroom, Justice Lawrence stirred to life and asked what had been said. When the witness repeated the word 'brothel' he still looked confused. Next to him, Biddle leant over and whispered, 'Brothel, Geoffrey, brothel'. Still failing to catch the word, Lawrence again asked what had been said. Leaning even closer, Biddle inadvertently switched his microphone on with his stomach and his words, 'Bordello, brothel, whorehouse', were broadcast to the assembled court.

The greatest weight of evidence presented by the prosecution had fallen on the military arm of the organisation, the Waffen SS. The defence adopted the strategy of distancing its activities from the rest of the SS by presenting evidence that, in the theatre of war, it fell under the overall command of the Wehrmacht. Moreover, as the war had progressed, its ranks were increasingly filled with transferred personnel and conscripts. One of the conditions the judges seemed likely to demand before declaring an organisation criminal would be that its membership was voluntary.

On 9 August the defence for the General Staff and High Command was heard. The prosecution had portrayed the group as integral to the implementation of Hitler's plans for waging aggressive war. The defence's argument was that the notion of the armed force's top officers as a discrete organisation had no basis in fact. The supposed members had never met together in one place at any time, and their implementation of Hitler's orders was not an act of conspiracy. It was obedience to the man who was both their Head of State and their Supreme Commander.

The defence's witnesses made up a stellar cast of Germany's elite commanders. Von Brauchitsch, von Manstein, and von Rundstedt all appeared on the stand to argue their sworn duty had been to follow their superiors' orders. Yet all three were mindful that they were likely to be put on trial themselves at a later date, and so were equally keen to demonstrate that they had chosen not to implement the most reprehensible of Hitler's policies. The cross-examining prosecution counsels were able to exploit this paradox to embarrassing effect.

The final organisation to have its case presented was the SA, popularly known as the Brownshirts. It was argued that it existed as a cohesive unit only up until the savage purge of its leadership in 1934. Thereafter, it became an umbrella organisation for a motley collection of subordinate groups. The largest of these was the Stahlhelm, an ex-servicemen's association, and defence provided witnesses to show that its members had been unwillingly co-opted into the SA.

Summing up for the prosecution, Thomas Dodd noted that, 'it is a strange feature of this trial that counsel for the respective organisations have not sought to deny these crimes but only to shift responsibility for their commission'. Yet the defence had also been sufficiently effective to exploit the doubts that existed in the minds of many of the lawyers at Nuremberg about the legality of criminalising a swathe of German society at a stroke.

On Saturday 31 August, a high sense of drama returned to the courtroom as the defendants made their final statements. As allowed under continental law, each defendant could, without being on oath, make a short speech. Lawrence had stipulated that each could last no longer than twenty minutes and should not repeat material or dispute evidence that hitherto had been presented by either the Prosecution or Defence counsels. For the members of the Tribunal, the assembled press, and spectators, there was an intense curiosity about the effect that ten months of horrific and damning evidence had had on the defendants. They themselves were acutely aware that this was their last opportunity to address the German people.

The men stood up in the dock in the order that their names appeared on the Indictment. Göring was thus the first to speak. After dismissing the Trial as a means to dispense justice, he flatly denied any prior knowledge of mass murders, claimed that he had neither expressed a desire to wage aggressive war, nor played any role in the outbreak of war. This was all too much for his co-defendant von Papen who accosted him during lunch and angrily demanded, 'Who in the world is responsible for all this destruction if not you?'

After Göring, there was an uneasy murmur in the courtroom as Rudolf Hess indicated that he wished to speak. Remaining in his seat, he embarked on a prepared speech, but after a few minutes began to ramble and repeat himself. The American prosecutor Telford Taylor called the performance a 'sad and ghoulish fiasco' and even Göring tugged at Hess's sleeve, imploring him to stop. At Lawrence's gentle insistence, Hess brought his speech to a close, and surprised everyone with a lucid and defiant coda:

'I was permitted to work for many years of my life under the greatest son whom my people has brought forth in its thousand-year history. Even if I could, I would not wish to erase this period of time from my existence. I am happy to know that I have done my duty to my people, my duty as a German, as a National Socialist, as a loyal follower of my Führer.'

On the witness stand Wilhelm Keitel had been one of the more forthright and penitent of the defendants. In his final speech he again spoke with dignity about his culpability:

'I believed, but I erred, and I was not in a position to

prevent what ought to have been prevented. That is my guilt. It is tragic to have to realise that the best I had to give as a soldier, obedience and loyalty, was exploited for purposes that could not be recognised at the time, and that I did not see that there is a limit even for a soldier's performance of his duty. That is my fate.'

The other military defendants were more bullish, with both Dönitz and Raeder arguing that the naval war had been conducted lawfully. Alfred Jodl claimed that he was guilty only of trying to do his job to the best of his ability, leading Judge Biddle to reflect, 'I am always struck by the apparently sincere and passionate idealism of so many of the defendants – but what ideals!'

Some of the defendants spoke of subjects beyond the remit of the trial. Hans Frank qualified the statement he had made during his defence that 'a thousand years would not suffice to erase the guilt brought upon our people', and argued that the guilt had already been erased by the crimes that the Allies had perpetrated against the German people. Albert Speer intoned a portentous warning against the dangers posed to civilisation by the increasingly devastating potential of modern weaponry.

Hjalmar Schacht had been stung by the insults thrown at him by Jackson, and responded in telling, if immodest, style:

'To be sure, I erred politically. I never claimed to be a politician, but my economic and financial policy of creating work by assisting credit proved brilliantly successful. My political mistake was not realising the extent of Hitler's criminal nature at an early enough time. But I did not stain my hands with one single illegal or immoral act.'

Of the remaining speeches, Arthur Seyss-Inquart made

the most measured. Whilst other defendants had wriggled and pointed fingers at others, most notably Hitler, Seyss-Inquart bravely stated:

'To me (Hitler) remains the man who made greater Germany a fact in German history. I served this man. And now? I cannot today cry, "Crucify him", since yesterday I cried, "Hosanna".'

The day ended with general relief, and indeed, a good deal of reluctant admiration for some of the defendants. Judge Birkett noted in his diary: 'This was a morning when the dignity of the trial may have been impaired by unseemly scenes: as it turned out, the dignity of the trial was enhanced by the defendants themselves'.

Lawrence closed proceedings by thanking the Defense Counsel for their assistance. After being in session for 216 days, the Tribunal was adjourned. It would not meet again until 30 September, when the judgement was to be announced.

Deliberations

As the judges began their deliberations, the humane decision was made to grant the defendants visits from their families. Although both Keitel and von Papen refused to let their loved ones see them in such disgrace, and efforts to contact Raeder's wife were stonewalled by the Soviets, both prisoners and guards found the presence of young children brightened the atmosphere. The prison's chaplain approached the young daughter of Alfred Rosenberg, and asked if she would like to join him in a prayer for her father. 'Don't give me that prayer crap,' was her trenchant reply.

At the same time as the conditions were slightly relaxed for the defendants, security for the judges was increased. All were issued with bullet-proof cars, and they were joined in their meetings by only two interpreters. The phone lines in the room were disconnected and after each session all scrap paper was removed and burnt. All eight judges joined in the discussions, although final judgment would pass to the four principals. Amid howls of protest from the Soviet contingent, it was agreed that a split vote would result in acquittal rather than conviction.

The first bone of contention was the applicability of Count One, the engaging in a conspiracy or common plan. The French judge, Donnedieu de Vabres, argued forcefully that the charge should be dropped. His contention was that conspiracy was not sufficiently defined in international law, that the charge was being applied retroactively and that, given the defendants were likely to be convicted on other grounds, it was an unnecessary piece of legal sophistry.

To a greater or lesser degree, all the other judges disagreed. Birkett was the most outspoken, arguing, 'If you say this dreadful war isn't planned, you bring about a national disaster. You acquit the party. Do you want to acquit the Nazi regime?' Acting as peacemaker, Francis Biddle suggested a compromise. He had not been convinced by the notion of a single, underlying plan behind all the crimes for which they had heard evidence. His argument was that the charge of conspiracy should not be applied to war crimes and crimes against humanity, but instead should be applied only to Count Two, the waging of aggressive war.

Biddle's suggestion won agreement, and the debate moved on to the date from which the conspiracy charge would be applied. The Hossbach conference of 5 November 1937 was chosen. This was the earliest instance in the trial's documentary record of Hitler's aggressive intentions toward the rest of Europe being expounded, but was relatively late in the history of the Nazi party. This would have a significant bearing on the judgements made against some of the older defendants.

The second contentious issue was the case against the organisations. Biddle was of the view that the trial had exposed manifold crimes that had been committed by individuals, but that group criminality had not been sufficiently established. Once again, Birkett questioned the effect on public opinion if the Tribunal was seen to exonerate the Gestapo or the SS. The French and Russian judges shared Birkett's fears. Biddle then mounted an extraordinary charm offensive to win his colleagues over to his view. The first step was to isolate those organisations for which there was a general consensus on acquittal. Bar the Soviets, all the judges felt that the cases against the Reich Cabinet and the High Command could be dropped, since both groups were relatively small and their members were senior enough to be called to account individually. Likewise, the overwhelming view was that the SA was too nebulous and impotent an organisation to convict.

Against the remaining organisations, Biddle achieved a hard-won compromise. His definition was that, for an organisation to be declared criminal, it must be 'formed or used in connection with the commission of crimes denounced by the charter'. But crucially, he also achieved agreement that exceptions to the wholesale guilty verdict would be 'persons who had no knowledge of the criminal purposes or acts of the organisation, and those who were drafted by the state for membership, unless they were personally implicated in the commission of acts declared criminal'.

This ruling was undoubtedly good news for the 'clerks, stenographers and janitors' to whom Jackson had referred, but the consequences for the Tribunal were huge. The case against the organisations had been weakened by the decision that the conspiracy charge would only be applied to Crimes against Peace (whatever crimes the Gestapo could be accused of plotting, the invasion of foreign countries did not number amongst them). Then Biddle inserted the compromise that, though a group could be declared criminal, it was not sufficient to brand all its members as criminals, and the guilt of those members could only be established in other trials. Thus Murray Bernays' founding concept of the International Military Tribunal as trying the whole Third Reich as one huge pre-meditated criminal plan, which was put into effect by the explicit connivance of the seven organisations, had been swept away by the judges. If nothing else it demonstrated that the trial was not a pre-determined act of vengeance by the Allied powers on their defeated enemy.

The Tribunal reconvened on Monday 30 September to an unprecedented level of security. Seats in the press gallery were at a premium, as global interest in the trial was re-ignited. After a stifling summer of often abstruse legal argument, the judgements were at hand. To the Tribunal staff who had sat in the courtroom for over ten months, the defendants had become familiar and even sympathetic characters. It was a chilling experience to watch as these men finally learnt if they would live or die.

A concern for due legal process rather than a sense of theatre meant that the judges spent the whole day taking turns to announce and explain their legal findings. It was a disappointment to the spectators but the defendants listened intently as the judges set out their belief that the Charter that contained the four charges was not 'an arbitrary exercise of power on the part of the victorious nations, but... the expression of international law existing at the time of its creation; and to that extent is itself a contribution to international law'. The criticism that the charge of waging aggressive war was being applied retroactively was dealt with at length by Biddle:

'To assert that it is unjust to punish those who in defiance of treaties and assurances have attacked neighbouring states without warning is obviously untrue, for in such circumstances the attacker must know that he is doing wrong, and so far from it being unjust to punish him, it would be unjust if his wrongs were allowed to go unpunished.'

Biddle then announced that every attack made by Germany against a neutral country, from the invasion of Poland in 1939 to the invasion of Russia in 1941, was deemed illegal.

Whilst this was no comfort to the military defendants, there was, according to von Papen, a palpable wave of relief in the dock when the ruling on Count One was announced. It was reckoned that, should the judges uphold the Prosecution's argument for a single, all-encompassing Nazi conspiracy, every defendant was doomed to hang. By limiting the conspiracy charge only to the waging of aggressive war, and its inception to 1937, the judges were seen to be holding out some hope of acquittals. This guarded optimism received a further boost when the judges ruled that only acts committed after 1939 would be considered in the judgements on War Crimes and Crimes against Humanity.

The judges ended the day with the verdicts on the organisations. The Leadership Corps was found guilty of participation in the slave labour programme, persecution of the Jews throughout Europe, and the ill-treatment of prisoners of war. The junior levels of the organisation were excluded from the judgement, as were individuals who had left the organisation before the outbreak of war.

The Gestapo and the SD were declared criminal organisations, although, again, low-level and clerical members were excluded from the judgement. A litany of atrocities was read out in the judgement against the SS, and the declaration of the organisation as criminal was perhaps the least surprising verdict in the trial. However those members of the Waffen SS who had been drafted into the organisation were exempted.

Of the defendants, only Göring showed surprise that the SA joined the Reich Cabinet and the High Command (General Staff) in not being declared illegal. The judgement ruled that, 'although in specific instances some units of the SA were used for the commission of War Crimes and Crimes against Humanity, it cannot be said that the members generally participated in or even knew of the criminal acts'. The Reich Cabinet and the General Staff & High Command were not declared criminal because the judges were not satisfied that they existed as discrete and coherent organisations. Despite this, the judges declared that individual members of those groups would be held accountable for their crimes, and spared the harshest words of the day for the senior military commanders of the General Staff:

'They have been responsible in large measure for the miseries and sufferings that have fallen on millions of men, women and children. They have been a disgrace to the honourable profession of arms… Although they were not a group falling within the words of the Charter, they were certainly a ruthless military caste.'

Reactions to the day's findings were mixed. The journalists and VIPs found the lack of drama anti-climatic, but several defendants left the courtroom feeling more hopeful than when they entered. For a day full of legal rulings, it was appropriate that its impact was most clearly seen by a lawyer. Dr von der Lippe excitedly noted that, 'The enemy No.1, the collective guilt idea embodied in the Indictment, is practically eliminated!'

The Verdicts on Individuals

Next morning, the judges laid out the structure of the day. The morning session would be spent delivering the verdicts on the individual defendants for the counts on which they had each been charged. The reasons for the verdicts would be summarised. Again, all four judges would read in turn to emphasise the international solidarity behind the decisions. In the afternoon, those convicted defendants would return to the dock one by one to hear their sentence. As had been the case throughout the entire trial, the wives and families of the defendants were not allowed in the courtroom, so had to huddle around radios to hear the fate of their loved ones broadcast to the nation.

Lawrence began proceedings with the judgement on

Göring. Finding him guilty of all four counts, Lawrence concluded:

'There is nothing to be said in mitigation. For Göring was often, indeed almost always, the moving force, both as political and as military leader; he was the director of the slave labour programme and the creator of the oppressive programme against the Jews and other races at home and abroad.'

Hess rocked back and forwards distractedly as his verdict was read. However bizarre his current behaviour, the judges believed that, 'there is nothing to show that he does not realise the nature of the charges against him or is incapable of defending himself'. In the Nazi hierarchy he was second only to Hitler and Göring, and colluded in the invasion of Czechoslovakia and Poland. He was found guilty on Counts One and Two.

To one journalist in the gallery Ribbentrop looked as if a noose was already around his neck. As a diplomat, he had played a key role in Nazi aggression and assisted in the deportation of French and Hungarian Jews: guilty on all four counts.

Keitel sat to attention at the mention of his name. 'Superior orders, even to a soldier, cannot be considered in mitigation where crimes so shocking and extensive have been committed': guilty on all four counts.

Kaltenbrunner had succeeded Heydrich as the head of the RHSA and, as such, had responsibility for the Gestapo and the Einsatzgruppen. The judges rejected Kaltenbrunner's claim that he was an innocent in Himmler's shadow: innocent of conspiring to wage war but guilty of War Crimes and Crimes against Humanity.

General Nikitchenko read the verdict on Rosenberg. He was a participant in the invasions of Norway and Russia, oversaw the seizure of 21,903 art objects from the defeated countries, and remained in office despite knowledge of the atrocities in the Occupied Eastern Territories. He was found guilty on all four counts.

Frank, it was conceded, had been out-manoeuvred by Himmler in implementing policies in occupied Poland, but he was a willing participant in the terrorism and deliberate starvation of the population. At the time he took up the post of Governor-General there were two and a half million Polish Jews. By the time he left only 100,000 remained. Frank was innocent of conspiracy, but guilty on Counts Three and Four.

De Vabres read the verdict on Frick, the 'chief Nazi administrative specialist and bureaucrat'. Remaining in his post despite knowledge of the crimes being committed in the concentration camps and complicit in the murder of the sick and the elderly, he was cleared of the conspiracy charge, but found guilty on the three other counts.

The verdict on Streicher was limited but damning. His 'incitement to murder and extermination at the same time when the Jews in the East were being killed under the most horrible conditions... constitutes a Crime against Humanity'.

Funk was not considered a senior enough figure in the Nazi hierarchy to be guilty under the charge of conspiracy, but his economic preparations for aggressive war brought a guilty verdict under Count Two. His participation in the slave labour programme and his knowledge of the valuables of murdered Jews being deposited in the Reichsbank under his control also won him guilty verdicts under Counts Three and Four.

Biddle read the verdict on Schacht's economic role in the rearmament of Germany. Rearmament in itself was not a crime under the terms of the Charter and the Prosecution had failed to convince the judges that he had clearly achieved this aim with the end of waging aggressive war in mind. As he was acquitted of all charges, he sat serenely amid the excited chatter that broke out in the courtroom, as if his exoneration had never been in doubt. He would later learn that his case had been a cause of vigorous disagreement among the judges, and he was the beneficiary of the hard won agreement that a 2-2 split would result in acquittal rather than conviction.

Dönitz was found not guilty under Count One as the judges accepted that he was not privy to plans to wage aggressive war. Moreover, the charges held that his conduct of the U-Boat war did not constitute a crime under the terms of the Charter. However, the judges ruled that his orders had violated the Treaty of London on submarine warfare and that he was guilty of passing on the Commando Order to the navy and seeking slave labour to work in the naval dockyards. Dönitz was visibly furious at being convicted under Counts Two and Three.

Dönitz had succeeded Raeder and where the former had been found not guilty under Count One, Raeder was convicted for his role in planning and implementing Hitler's aggressive aims. To the guilty verdicts under Counts One and Two was added a conviction under Count Three for passing on the Commando Order.

Von Schirach was charged under Counts One and Four.

The judges ruled that neither he nor the Hitler Youth he had commanded played any part in the conspiracy to wage aggressive war. However von Schirach's other role as Reich Governor in Vienna and his complicity in the deportation of 60,000 Viennese Jews to Poland brought a guilty verdict under Count Four.

The verdict on Sauckel was swift, with the charges under Counts One and Two dismissed for lack of evidence. However his responsibility for the slave labour programme 'which he carried out under terrible conditions of cruelty and suffering' ensured his guilt under Counts Three and Four.

Jodl was told that 'he cannot now shield himself behind the myth of soldierly obedience at all costs'. For drawing up plans to wage aggressive war, advising Hitler on strategy and operations, and passing on the Commando and Commissar orders, he was found guilty on all four counts.

Like Schacht, von Papen had been charged under Counts One and Two. The judges were similarly unconvinced that the assistance he gave Hitler in his accession to power was done with knowledge of the latter's aggressive aims. Therefore, von Papen was found not guilty and was told that he would be discharged when the Tribunal adjourned.

Seyss-Inquart had little hope of a similar outcome. Throughout the trial he remained loyal to Hitler and expressed no regret for his own actions. Despite governing the Netherlands with less arbitrary brutality than the rulers of other occupied territories, he was judged not guilty under Count One but guilty on the other three counts.

Speer was charged on all four counts but, because of his relatively late entry into the Nazi government, he was swiftly acquitted under Counts One and Two. He knew that

Sauckel would meet his demands for workers through slave labour, and was aware that concentration camp inmates and prisoners of war were forced to work in the arms industries. He was found guilty under Counts Three and Four, although the judges did record in mitigation Speer's opposition to Hitler's scorched earth policy.

Like Speer, von Neurath was charged on all four counts. Preceding von Ribbentrop as Minister of Foreign Affairs, he was adjudged to have conspired in the waging of aggressive war. In his later role as Reich Protector of Bohemia and Moravia he was found guilty of War Crimes and Crimes against Humanity. However, the mitigating factors that the judges mentioned in their verdict implied that the conviction under all four counts might not be as deadly for him as it would be for other defendants.

The judges were not convinced by the Prosecution's argument that Fritzsche's propaganda broadcasts were intended to incite the German people to commit atrocities, and therefore he could not be said to have participated in War Crimes and Crimes against Humanity. Too junior to found guilty under the charge of conspiracy, Fritzsche became the third defendant to be acquitted.

Nikitchenko ended the session with the verdict on the absent Bormann. He was declared not guilty under Count One, of conspiracy, but guilty for Counts Three and Four, of war crimes and crimes against humanity.

Sentencing

Three of the defendants (Schacht, von Papen and Fritzsche) had, of course, been acquitted and escaped the necessity of returning to the courtroom to hear sentence passed on them. Instead they were faced by the bizarre charade of a press conference in front of dozens of journalists. Many believed that the men had been lucky to be acquitted. Rebecca West recorded a commonly held view that Schacht and von Papen, 'old foxes' who 'had tricked and turned and doubled and laid doggo all their lives,' had fooled everyone again. There was hostility both within the press conference and outside the building. Fearing that a lynch mob was gathering, the three acquitted men chose to spend their first night of official freedom within the jail.

The other defendants returned on the afternoon of 1 October to hear their fates. After a heart-stopping false start during which the headphones carrying the translations failed, the eighteen men, beginning with Göring, stood to receive their sentences. Four were given imprisonment for periods ranging from ten to 20 years. Karl Dönitz, who had briefly succeeded Hitler as Chancellor, was sentenced to 10 years' imprisonment in Spandau prison. Constantin von Neurath received a sentence of 15 years. Both Baldur von Schirach, former head of the Hitler Youth, and Albert Speer, Hitler's architect and Minister of Armaments, were sentenced to 20 years in Spandau. Three of the defendants — Hess, who seemed almost oblivious to what was going on around him, Raeder and Funk — received life sentences.

All the other defendants — Göring, Frank, Frick, Streicher, Sauckel, Jodl, von Ribbentrop, Keitel, Kaltenbrunner, Rosenberg, Seyss-Inquart and the absent Bormann — were sentenced to death by hanging. Apart from Frank who murmured an incongruous, 'Thank you', after hearing sentence, the judge's words were received in silence. Back in their cells, the men had time to reflect on the sentences.

Carrying Out the Sentences

One of the defendants was determined to avoid the fate the court had assigned him. At about a quarter to eleven on the night before the scheduled execution, a prison guard, glancing through the hatch in Göring's door, saw that the former Reichsmarschall was twitching and moaning on his bed. He appeared to be having a heart attack but, when the door was unlocked and a doctor summoned to examine him, it became clear that he had crushed a cyanide capsule in his mouth. Within minutes Göring was dead. Rumours about how he gained access to a suicide pill would circulate for years. In 2005 a 78-year-old former guard at Nuremberg confessed that he had been duped by a pretty German girl into smuggling medicine into the prison for the ailing Nazi.

Despite Göring cheating the allies of the chance to execute him, the executions of the other men went ahead as planned. They were to take place in the prison gymnasium that stood next to the cell building in which they were all held. The defendants who had received prison sentences were still in the jail. Speer records his irritation at the sounds of hammering and sawing in the night and his sudden realisation that they were putting up the gallows. At one in the morning on 16 October 1946 the men who were to hang, now ten in number, began to move from the cells, down the corridor, down the outside stairs and across the yard to the gymnasium. The first to meet his fate was von Ribbentrop. He entered the execution chamber at eleven minutes past one. His hands were still manacled and now the cuffs were removed and replaced with a leather strap. Originally, it had been intended that the condemned men should walk to their executions with their hands free but, following Göring's suicide, the authorities were taking no chances. Von Ribbentrop, regaining the dignity he had lost during the trial, approached the steps of the scaffold with apparent stoicism. Standing on the scaffold with his arms and legs tied, he spoke his last words. 'God protect Germany. Thank God that He is merciful. My last wish is that Germany realize its entity and that an understanding be reached between the East and the West. I wish peace to the world.'

Keitel was the next to enter the chamber, approaching the second scaffold only minutes after von Ribbentrop died on the first. With von Ribbentrop's body still concealed inside the first scaffold, Keitel mounted the gallows and made his own last statement. 'I call on God Almighty to have mercy on the German people. More than 2 million German soldiers went to their death for the fatherland before me. I follow now my sons – all for Germany.'

The other defendants followed in the order of indictment. Kaltenbrunner, Rosenberg, Frank, Frick, Streicher, Sauckel, Jodl. Each man was allowed a brief final statement. Most committed their souls to God and expressed their hopes for the future greatness of Germany. Streicher, still wrapped in his paranoid fantasies, assured his executioners that 'the Bolsheviks will get you' and then died with the name of his wife, Adele, on his lips. Sauckel, angry enough to kick the door as he entered the execution chamber, proclaimed his own innocence and the injustice of the sentence.

The last to die was Seyss-Inquart. 'I hope this execution is the last act of the tragedy of the Second World War,' he proclaimed, 'and that the lessons of this war will make for peace and understanding among the peoples. I believe in Germany.' Then the noose and the black hood were placed over his head and he too was executed.

All the bodies of the condemned men were now placed in their coffins and Göring's corpse was brought to join them. As the sun came up on the morning of the 16th, two vans, with an escort of jeeps, took the bodies away. No formal announcement about their eventual disposal was ever made beyond the blunt statement that the eleven men had been cremated and their ashes scattered. Rumours spread that the bodies had been taken to the gas ovens at the Dachau concentration camp and cremated there, which would have had a terrible appositeness, but it seems likely that the ashes were scattered at some still unidentified site in Germany. At the end of months of judicial inquiry, culminating in the sentencing and execution of the eleven men, the very last thing the Allies wanted was to provide a grave for reverent pilgrimage by unrepentant Nazis.

Epilogue

For the three men who were acquitted at Nuremberg, their freedom was short-lived. Schacht, Fritzsche and von Papen were all re-arrested by the new German authorities and tried as part of the de-Nazification process. All three were given prison sentences, although none served a long time behind bars. Fritzsche was released in the autumn of 1950 and died of cancer three years later. His memoirs provide interesting insights into the Nuremberg trial from the perspective of a defendant. Both Schacht and von Papen, the 'two old foxes' who had 'tricked and turned and doubled and laid doggo all their lives,' as Rebecca West described them, were released in the late 1940s and went on to have long and prosperous lives in the new Germany. Von Papen died in 1969 at the age of 89. The 93-year-old Schacht died the following year.

Those who were sentenced to terms of imprisonment at the trial stayed on in cells in the Nuremberg jail until July 1947 when they were transferred to Spandau prison on the outskirts of Berlin. A 19th century building intended to hold 600 men, Spandau became home to just seven and, throughout the 1950s, this number dwindled. Von Neurath, suffering from ill health, was released in 1954 and died two years later. Raeder, his sentence reduced and also in poor health, followed him out of the gates of Spandau in 1955. Having served his full term, Dönitz left the prison the following year and, in 1957, Walther Funk's life sentence was reduced because of his deteriorating health and he was released. The two youngest defendants at Nuremberg, Albert Speer and Baldur von Schirach, served out their full sentences of 20 years and were both released in 1966. This left only one prisoner in Spandau. By most standards of justice, Rudolf Hess, old, confused and probably insane, should have also qualified for release by the 1960s but the Russians were determined that he should live out his life behind bars. The last of the prisoners tried at Nuremberg died in 1987 at the age of 93, reportedly by suicide. Speculation about Hess continues to this day. Elaborate conspiracy theories arguing that the man imprisoned at Spandau was not the real Hess but a double are dismissed by most historians, as are neo-Nazi claims that he was eventually murdered, but it does seem rather unlikely that a senile and mentally ill man in his nineties could have ended his life without assistance.

The Nuremberg Trial, although it proved to be the only trial of Nazi war criminals to be conducted by an international tribunal, was not the end of efforts to bring those who had committed crimes against humanity to justice. Trials at Nuremberg continued for more than two years. The Americans conducted a dozen trials between December 1946 and April 1949, including the trial of twenty three doctors accused of medical experimentation in the concentration camps (seven of the doctors were eventually executed) and the trial of officers from the Einsatzgruppen, the death squads which had operated in Eastern Europe. Hundreds of war criminals were tried by military courts in the Russian, French, British and American zones of occupied Germany in the immediate post-war years. Other men and (occasionally) women accused of crimes were tried in the countries where the crimes had been committed. In 1947, for example, a court in Poland sentenced Rudolf Hoess, the camp commandant at Auschwitz, to death. The hunt to bring Nazi war criminals to justice continued. (Indeed, it still continues to this day.) The most dramatic trials in the decades after Nuremberg have probably been those of Adolf Eichmann in Jerusalem in 1961 and of Klaus Barbie in Lyon in 1987 but there have been many others.

The trial at Nuremberg, however, will always remain the most historically significant of all the war trials. Not only were the defendants the most senior Nazis ever brought before a court. Not only were the charges brought against them the most wide-ranging and comprehensive criminal indictments served on Hitler's regime and its supporters. The Nuremberg Trial was a test of the ability of victorious nations to deal justly with the vanquished. Many claimed that this was impossible. Most of the defendants, unsurprisingly, believed that the trial was revenge masquerading as justice. Göring, in particular, was contemptuous of what he sneeringly called 'victors' justice'. Others, less personally implicated in the charges, were concerned that they had no basis in international law. Yet, viewed with the hindsight of sixty years, the Nuremberg Trial does seem to have fulfilled many of the hopes of those who determined that it should take place. Justice *was* seen to be done. Robert Jackson's belief that the Allies, 'flushed with victory and stung with injury,' would 'stay the hand of vengeance and voluntarily submit their captive enemies to the judgment of the law' was largely confirmed. In its attempts to re-establish the rule of law, the Nuremberg Trial, if not unflawed, proved a necessary and admirable conclusion to six years of brutal and terrible warfare.

Further Reading

Coates, Tim (ed), *The Judgement of Nuremberg, 1946*, London: Uncovered Editions, 1999

Conot, Robert E., *Justice at Nuremberg*, London: Weidenfeld & Nicolson, 1983

Gaskin, Hilary, *Eyewitnesses at Nuremberg*, London: Arms & Armour Press, 1990

Gilbert, G. M., *Nuremberg Diaries*, London: Eyre & Spottiswoode, 1948

Neave, Airey, *Nuremberg*, London: Hodder & Stoughton, 1978

Persico, Joseph, *Nuremberg: Infamy on Trial*, London: Allison & Busby, 1995

Smith, Bradley F., *Reaching Judgement at Nuremberg*, London: Andre Deutsch, 1977

Speer, Albert, *Spandau: The Secret Diaries*, London: Collins, 1976

Taylor, Telford, *The Anatomy of the Nuremberg Trials*, New York: Knopf, 1992

Tusa, Ann and Tusa, John, *The Nuremberg Trial*, London: Macmillan, 1983

West, Rebecca, *A Train of Powder*, London: Macmillan, 1955

Websites

www.law.umkc.edu/faculty/projects/ftrials/nuremberg/
nuremberg.htm
www.yale.edu/lawweb/avalon/imt/imt.htm
www.nizkor.org/hweb/imt/tgmwc/
Three sites which gather together documents and testimony
from the trial.

www.jewishvirtuallibrary.org
Contains much valuable material on the Holocaust and on
the trials of Nazi war criminals.

www.spartacus.schoolnet.co.uk
A general history site which includes short biographies of
both defendants and prosecutors and short extracts from
significant documents.

Index

Also available in this series

Current

Nelson by Victoria Carolan 1 904048 54 4
Secret Societies by Nick Harding 1 904048 41 2
St George by Giles Morgan 1 904048 57 9
The Cathars by Sean Martin 1 904048 33 1
The Crusades by Michael Paine 1 904048 38 2
The Holy Grail by Giles Morgan 1 904048 34 X
The Knights Templar by Sean Martin 1 904048 28 5

Forthcoming

Alchemy & Alchemists by Sean Martin
 – new edition 1 904048 62 5
Jack the Ripper by Whitehead & Rivett
 – new edition 1 904048 69 2
Nazi War Trials by Andrew Walker
 – new title 1 904048 50 1
Roget: A Biography by Nick Rennison
 – new title 1 904048 64 1
The Gnostics by Sean Martin
 – new title 1 904048 56 0

Price £9.99

Available from Bookshops or via our website
www.pocketessentials.com

Pocket Essentials, P.O. Box 394, Harpenden, Herts, AL5 1XJ

The Nuremberg Prisoners Sentenced: The twenty-one defendants at Nu
International Tribunal on the morning of 1st October, to hear the verdict
to death): Rudolf Hess (life imprisonment): Joachim Von Ribbentrop (de
Rosenberg (death): Hans Frank (death): Wilhelm Frick (death): Julius
(acquitted and liberated). Back Row, from left to right: Grand Admiral Ka
Schirach (twenty years imprisonment): Fritz Sauckel (death): Alfred Jodl
(twenty years imprisonment): Constantin von Neurath (fifteen years impr